What People Say About

"Thank you, Rhoberta, for the wonderful mes
ponder life in different eyes." – Anita

"I just wanted to thank you for the Optimize ezine which I subscribe to. I truly find it to be a great source of inspiration and encouragement. I have been a positive thinker (as opposed to a positive do-er!) for 50 years. Since reading your e-mails, I feel as if a giant bear, which has been hibernating within me, is beginning to stir—and I'm excited at the prospect of my own potential! Well done and keep up the excellent work." - Trevor

"It really has helped me a lot over the last ...how long has it been, 2 years? Well, long enough for me to start noticing what a positive effect you've had on me!"
– Helen, Nova Scotia

"What a great perspective!" – Jim

"Thank you for your quotes and tips for Optimal Living. I really appreciate them. I like how practical and applicable they are to my daily world. Often what you have written is just the thing to help me sort my unspoken thoughts and assist me to clear my frustrations. Bless your heart!" – Catherine

"I read all of your messages, because they are vitamins of the mind for me. As you are aware, in order to change a habit, or except a new idea, you must feed that information into your mind continuously, until your old ideas leave, and you accept the new ideas. The other key is to get different perspectives on the same ideas, and that is why I enjoy your work so much." - Bob

"What a refreshing and uplifting experience!! I loved this book! I am going to recommend it to my friends. I especially liked [Dr. Shaler's] thoughts on learning from others."
– Michelle Clancy

Optimize Your Day!

Practical Wisdom for Optimal Living

Live fully now!
Rhoberta Shaler

Rhoberta Shaler, Ph.D.

www.OptimizeLifeNow.com

Although the author, editor and publisher have made every effort to ensure the accuracy and completeness of information contained herein, we assume no responsibility for errors, inaccuracies, omissions, or inconsistencies. We would appreciate receiving feedback on any of the above so they can be addressed in future printings. Please use the contact information below.

Rhoberta Shaler, PhD
OPTIMIZE YOUR DAY!
Practical Wisdom for Optimal Living
ISBN: 0-9711689-0-3

Cover design and book layout by Kera McHugh
somethingelse web+graphics, www.time4somethingelse.com

Cover Photo © 2000, Rhoberta Shaler, PhD. Taken in Sukhothai, Thailand.
Back Cover Photo of Dr. Shaler © 2000 Nicholas Seiflow, Vancouver, BC Canada

2nd Edition First Printing: September, 2001; Second Printing: October 2002
Printed in the United States of America

Published by People Skills Press, San Diego CA

For information, contact:
Rhoberta Shaler, PhD
Optimize Life Now, San Diego CA
Email: info@OptimizeLifeNow.com
Website: www.OptimizeLifeNow.com

TABLE OF CONTENTS

A different world cannot be created by indifferent people.

- author unknown

Optimize Your Day!

To 'optimize' is to make as effective and functional as possible. Is that what you want for each day of your life?

Living optimally is about creating awareness, not pressure. A day of work and a day of rest can be equally effective and rewarding. Knowing what you want to be, do and have, and moving in that direction consciously each day, is Optimal Living.

Personal success is respecting what is significant, important and valuable to you. Demonstrating that respect with your behavior honors those relationships, activities, environments and values. Your behavior is your secret to Sustainable Success.

In order to create the life you say you want, you may need to make some changes. This may take some work. Remember, if those changes were easy, you would have done them already! At any time, simply ask yourself if what you are doing or not doing is moving you forward or filling time. Alter your course accordingly.

Some concepts are offered in several ways in this book. There is a good reason for that. Folks often have to meet the same information many times in varied ways before they take action.

There is no magic! If you truly want the life you say you want, you will gently turn in the direction of your goals and eliminate thoughts, activities and habits that keep you from moving forward. Each moment you are making choices. Make them wisely.

What is important is simple:
Know what you value and spend your time accordingly.
This is integrity and it will bring you peace.

I wish you well.

Rhoberta Shaler

Rhoberta Shaler, PhD, San Diego, CA

From The Author...

This book is the product of years of learning and growth. I am pleased and proud to have the opportunity of a third printing!

I thank my family, friends and colleagues for their many, many gifts of time, feedback, experiences, support and insights – which are the very richness of my life and thus the content of this book.

I particularly thank my husband, Keith Couch, for his constant love that lights me up; and my editor, designer and right hand, Kera McHugh, for her creativity, skill and willingness to go the extra mile to capture the essence of my work.

I would love to hear comments and stories from readers of this book. If you would take the time to send me your thoughts, I will keep them for future reference and possible inclusion in further books.

Please find my postal address at www.OptimizeLifeNow.com under 'Contact Us' or email me at RS@OptimizeLifeNow.com

Make it a great day!

Rhoberta Shaler, PhD
October 2002

Consider carefully.
Write thoughtfully.

Optimize Your Day!

Perceptions...

If you are distressed by anything external, the pain is not due to the thing itself, but to your estimate of it and this you have the power to revoke at any moment. — Marcus Aurelius

Perception is everything. You choose what meaning you give to events, situations, and circumstances. That is such a powerful realization. You choose how you respond with your feelings, your words, and your actions. Choice is powerful.

Are you exercising your choices? Some folks don't. It is the difference between grabbing hold of the side of the boat with white knuckles while letting someone else steer, and, taking the helm yourself and choosing the destination and the route. It is the difference between seeing yourself as an "effect" or a "cause". Which position do you prefer?

Sometimes people say that events were beyond their control. Some very few events seem to be, however, you can always control your view of the situation and your response to it. Even in stories of concentration camp life, the survivors were often the ones who refused to be beaten down, refused to starve, refused to hate. They made strong choices, didn't they? You can, too.

“I must do something" is a much stronger statement than "Something must be done". Do you go along on someone else's ride meanwhile feeling resentful and unfulfilled? Do you take the helm, chart your course, reach your destination and celebrate? It's your choice, isn't it?

Spend an hour writing in your journal about how you would like to feel at this time next year. Ask yourself what would give you that feeling and what you are willing to do to have it. Write that down, too.

This writing will be the blueprint for living the best year of your life.

Planting Seeds...

Don't judge each day by the harvest you reap, but by the seeds you plant.
— Robert Louis Stevenson

What kind of seeds are you planting in your life? Are you careful and thoughtful about where you plant them? Are you willing to take the time and energy to nourish and cultivate the soil, or do you just stick the seeds in and hope for the best? Do you scatter them freely or choose your plot carefully? Do you take the time to consider and compare seeds and choose only the best for your garden at this time?

Is your focus on planting well or on harvesting? Clearly, it is the planting that produces the harvest.

Do you ask for help from a master gardener? When you want someone to do something for you or to help you, do you care enough to ask forthrightly, or do you put out subtle hints and hope he or she will pick them up and offer to help you? Asking directly for help is a demonstration of health. Your own self-concept is secure enough to say, "I need/want help". You show respect for the knowledge and/or skills of your friend or colleague. You are willing to hear "Yes" or "No" and continue the relationship. Then, you feel no need to pretend you do not need help when you do.

Plant carefully. It's your harvest!

...Planting Seeds

Think about what you really want to do, be or have. Think of all the people you know who might be able to help you have, be or do those things. Choose whom to approach and ask them to help you. Cultivate the soil. Sow the seeds. Prepare for the harvest.

What's Your Passion?

The trick in life is to decide what's your major aim—to be rich, a golf champion, world's best father (mother), etc. Once that's settled, you can get on with the happy orderly task of achieving it. — Stanley Goldstein

Finding your passions in life—the things you want to do most, that feed you, that bring you joy, that nurture your soul—is the most important starting point. Most people are very busy making a living and seldom consider if they are passionate about what they are doing. Certainly, at times, putting the food on the table is the major consideration, however, there is nothing to stop you from considering the larger question in your leisure hours.

What would it be like to spend 85% of your time involved in doing things that bring you satisfaction and joy? If that sounds appealing, why not find out what it is and get on with it as quickly as possible. Why postpone your life?

What's Your Passion?

Take some time to list the things that nurture, nourish and support you. Are they things you do daily or, at least, weekly? Make a plan to do one good thing for yourself daily. Each morning, before you get out of your bed, decide which of those wonderful things you will do for yourself each day.

You deserve love and respect.

Begin by giving it to yourself every day.

Bring Happiness...

We must have courage to bet on our ideas, to take the calculated risk, and to act. Everyday living requires courage if life is to be effective and bring happiness. — Maxwell Maltz

Do you act on your dreams? No, not the dreams you have while sleeping, but rather the dreams you have for what you might do or become. Do you have a list of things you want to accomplish in your lifetime? That's the beginning. Some folks are afraid to dream, afraid to aim high. Are you?

The beginning of accomplishment is the clear idea of what it is you want to do. Clarity is the most important component. You know that your goals have to be S-M-A-R-T— Specific, Measurable, Attainable, Realistic, and Time-Bounded. If someone has done it somewhere, sometime, it is attainable. Realistic is not a limiter. It simply means that wanting to actually run a marathon on your own two legs if your own two legs are missing is unrealistic, whereas wheeling a marathon is attainable. Have SMART goals.

So, what's stopping you? Once you determine the direction of your dream, start walking. You may have to take baby steps at first. You will have to make a plan, a map that will take you from where you presently are to where you want to go. Then, map in hand, set out. You can do this! Just begin.

Think back to the things you dreamed of doing in your teens and early twenties. What did you want to accomplish? Have you done any of those things?

What do you want most right now?

Are you willing to use your time and money to accomplish those things? I hope so; otherwise, they are simply wishes waiting for magic to fulfill them. You have to be your own magic if you really want something.

Clarify what you want in every detail. Make a plan to achieve it. Follow the plan, no matter what. It may not be easy but it certainly is simple. Get going!

Impact...

If you think you are too small to have an impact, try going to bed with a mosquito in the room. — Anita Roddick

Most overnight successes take years to accomplish. Any person in the music, science, entertainment or art field will attest to that, for sure. How did it happen? One small step at a time.

You have probably heard the saying attributed to a Chinese philosopher who said that the journey of a thousand miles begins with the first step. You've also probably heard many times that the squeaky wheel gets the grease. So, putting these two thoughts together, you could say that continuing to move forward while asking for what you need and want is a good way to get where you're going and to get what you want, right?

Learning to break large goals down into manageable chunks means knowing how to eat an elephant—one spoonful at a time! This is so easy to forget.

Big, big plans, dreams, visions and goals, important though they are, can leave you feeling overbooked, overworked, and overwhelmed if you do not take the time to create the "daily do-ables"—the sub-goals. You know the joy and satisfaction of setting the day's goals and meeting them. You cannot be prepared for a marathon in one day. Some folks beat themselves up because they have not reached their potential—their BIG goal—and forget that, just like the marathon, success is built on progress. It means incremental training every week.

Take your biggest dream and subdivide it into 'daily do-ables'
— pieces you know you can accomplish.

Start eating that elephant one spoonful at a time!

It is a common experience that a problem difficult at night is resolved in the morning after the committee of sleep has worked on it.
— John Steinbeck

One very important strategy for creating a life that works the way you want it to is extreme self-care. For some people, self-care might be just doing whatever it takes to stay alive and somewhat presentable. For others, self-care might include regular trips to the dentist or massage therapist, and other preventative practices. But EXTREME self-care, what is this?

Extreme self-care means really knowing what makes you feel your best...and doing it! It means being in tune with the changes in your mood and your ability to function optimally, noticing the signs that you are less than at your best and doing something about it. Specifically, this may mean ensuring that you have enough sleep each night. Planning your time to include your exercise program and to provide yourself with excellent nutrition. Providing yourself with interesting challenges and nourishing activities. And, pampering yourself!

If you just dismissed the notion of pampering yourself with a roll of your eyes, this may be a signal that your self-esteem needs buffing. Taking good care of yourself allows you to have something to give in your relationships, in your career, in fact, everywhere that is important to you.

It's like putting money in the bank!

Reflect on the time that you spend taking extremely good care of yourself. Distinguish between the time spent on "looking good for others" and that spent "feeling good about yourself". When you approve of yourself, when you are on track with what is valuable to you, you will look good AND have something valuable to give.

Doing What Is Right...

Nothing is more important than doing what is right. That is so absurdly obvious that most people pay no attention to it. Most people seem to think that what is obvious is beneath them. They pass up truth in favor of something more intellectually stimulating. — Paul Williams

"Doing the right thing" is such an interesting, and ambiguous, phrase. Only you know what is right for you. It begins with knowing what you believe and value and, then, behaving accordingly.

Doing what is right means not *intentionally* hurting yourself or anyone else, too. Sometimes, to do what is right may seem to cause someone pain, or, more likely, to cause someone to *decide* they are in pain. While your child is screaming with anger, it is sometimes difficult to explain to them that it is right that they cannot take another child's toys home. When your best friend asks you for your "honest" opinion of their actions, a delicate balance is required. Use good communication skills. Be totally honest and totally kind simultaneously. It is often the way that something is said, rather than the content, that causes pain. Most people can hear most things if care is taken in the way they are expressed.

Being true to your own values may require relinquishing your need for the approval of others. This is the moment of truth for many folks. What is right for you, what is in integrity for you, is the action that will bring you peace.

...Doing What Is Right

Reflect on choices that you have made that did not "sit" well with you. Was that because you were not doing what was right for you? What changes might you have made to the situation to make it right for you? Practice mentally what you will do if the situation arises again. How can you be totally kind and totally honest at the same time?

Backbone...

In achieving success, backbone is more important than wishbone.
— Frank Tyger

Do you begin each day by remembering your three top goals? Can you bring those three top goals to mind instantly? If not, it will be very difficult to achieve them.

The degree of clarity you have, knowing exactly where you are heading, creates momentum that takes you through to completion. Without that, you may well meander, sidestep and procrastinate unconsciously. You may choose to meander, slow down, rest, reflect, or rethink, however, the point is to do it consciously.

Why is it so important to have goals? That's simple—would you go to the travel agent and take any ticket they gave you? No, you have a destination in mind and you purchase only that ticket. You know where you want to go and you make sure that's where your ticket will take you. Life is the same. Some people think that this does not allow for spontaneity. Of course it does! You decide on the speed at which you take your journey to any given goal. You can choose Lear jet, train, bus or tramp steamer. Sometimes you want to get there very quickly, other times you're happy to arrive there with ample time to see all the sights along the way. The whole point is to truly understand that you are choosing how you take the journey.

Spend some time assessing your travel plans. If you're still being jostled in the ticket line up, feeling pushed this way and that by other travelers, choose differently. Decide on your destination, purchase your ticket, pack your bags and then happy trails!

Achievement...

The greatest achievement of the human spirit is to live up to one's opportunities and make the most of one's resources. — Vauvenargues

Many times, you feel as though you are stuck. You may complain to friends that you could do what you want to do, "if only...". It is so convenient to have something seemingly beyond your control to keep you from your dreams, isn't it?

I think there are three things in life--needs, wants and wishes—and it is imperative to know the differences among them. Needs are obvious. These are the basics of life that allow you to continue to live—air, water, shelter, food. Wishes are those things that you say you want but are completely unwilling to do anything about creating or attracting to you. Wants are those things you have a passion for, a desire strong enough to compel you to take action and stay on the path towards the goal until you achieve it.

It is very important, then, to reflect honestly, to distinguish between your wishes and your wants. If something is only a wish, there is no need to complain about not having it. If it is truly a 'want', you will be motivated to take steps, no matter how small, to achieve it.

For today, choose to focus on your wants and use your energy there. Make a list of your wishes, too. Wishes may become wants as you give them attention and arrange your time to accommodate them.

Look For The Good...

Look for the good things, not the faults. It takes a good deal bigger-sized brain to find out what is not wrong with people and things than to find out what is wrong. — R.L. Sharpe

Catch them doing something right! Decide to focus on what you see, hear, feel, touch, taste and smell that is pleasing. Look for something good in every situation.

It is so easy to criticize. It's likely that you learned all about it when you were young. "Don't do that!", "Let me do it for you so it will be done right.", "Who do you think you are?", "That's such a silly thing to say." We learn by example. Can you remember a person who was always ready to catch you doing something right?

It is important to your health in every way to become an encourager. Encouragers find the good in you and move it forward. They shine a spotlight on what you are doing well, 'Encouragement' means to inspire with courage, spirit or hope. You can encourage yourself. Is your self-talk encouraging? Do you encourage others?

Notice today how you talk to yourself. When you are sitting waiting anywhere today—at a stoplight, on eternal hold on the telephone, at the doctor's—spend that time reminding yourself that you are the "chooser" of your self-concept. What are you choosing to tell yourself? If you would like a more encouraging message...CHANGE IT!

Begin Wherever You Are...

Every successful man [and woman] I have heard of has done the best he could with conditions as he [she] found them. — Edgar Watson Howe

One of the common ways you put off starting your plans or projects may be to wait for the optimal conditions. In a singles seminar I used to give, I said that many people believe that when they've paid off their debts, lost twenty pounds, cleaned our their basements and "fill in the blank", THEN, they seem sure that they will be ready for a relationship. Many folks are like that about many of their visions or dreams. The time is never quite right. The conditions could be better. The money could be more abundant or available.

You have the opportunity to use every 24-hour period in the way you choose. At some level, you've chosen it. If you think it through, you may be choosing to pay the rent rather than choosing to go out for the evening. Nevertheless, it IS a choice. You can choose to take a step towards your dreams every day. It may be spending ten minutes visualizing your dream as reality, or it may be learning a skill you will need—whatever it is, you can choose to do it!

...Begin Wherever You Are

Is there something that you are planning to do when the time is right? Do you know what those "right" conditions are? Do you really have to wait or is this just an acceptable reason to put off stretching to reach your goals? You can become so very clever at creating logical reasons why you cannot be, do and have what you say you want that even YOU believe it! Examine this for yourself and see if you are keeping good things for yourself "on hold"!

Excess, upon occasion, can be exhilarating, because it prevents moderation from acquiring the deadening effect of a habit.
— Somerset Maugham

Is "balanced spontaneity" an oxymoron? If you are spontaneous most of the time, you may feel, and be, out of control. If you are seldom spontaneous, you may be too contained for your own good. It is the balance that is the important issue, isn't it?

My grandson, Luka, and I used to have a treat. We would buy something he loved to eat and he would say, "Nana, let's eat it all gone!" and we would do just that! Usually, it was ice cream. It may have been just a double serving but it would seem like such marvelous excess and extravagance. You can have this same feeling by giving yourself a day off, an afternoon off, or an hour of enjoying something special. It also can be delicious to just take a half-hour nap exactly when you need one.

For one person, taking a nap is excess, giving in, being lazy. To another, it is listening to the needs of the body. The good news is that there is no right answer. The call is for honesty. If you are seriously avoiding completing a task, "listening to your body's need for a nap" becomes very welcome, if not miraculously convenient. If you are truly very tired, taking the nap might be just the thing to ensure that the project gets done. It is all part of your willingness to tell the truth to yourself.

Take a few moments to reflect on the last time you chose to argue with yourself over a choice you were about to make. Which part of you won? Was it the part that held onto your highest resolves or the part that led you to feel that you had given in again? Write down a phrase that you could say to yourself the next time this happens to remind you to choose in favor of your highest intentions. It could be something like, "Keep my eyes on the prize" or "I am my own best friend". You'll create the perfect phrase for yourself... then use it, every time!

Most people would rather die than think, in fact, they do that.
— Bertrand Russell

Bertrand Russell was well known for speaking his mind clearly and straightforwardly and in this quote, he certainly did so. Whether or not you agree with him entirely is of little matter. What matters, I think, is that you ask yourself if you are truly engaging in thinking for yourself.

Do you ask yourself tough questions? Do you question why you do things? Are you willing to look at the things you do for approval …and whose approval it is you're after and why? Do you ask yourself if you are moving in the direction of your highest dreams? Are you kind? Do your actions match what you say is important to you?

This, to me, is the "thinking" that Russell speaks of. Enquire into what you are doing and why. Are you creative, conscious and moving forward or simply standing still or treading water? Staying awake in your life will bring you closer to the results you want to create.

Spend some time answering the questions in today's tip. Most people seem to avoid time alone, and, avoid asking themselves questions about their motives even more.

If you want to have a more fulfilling and satisfying life, then you must examine your life. There is no escaping this. If exceptional is better than acceptable to you, then ask yourself those tough questions and use the answers to soar!

Believing...

The thing always happens that you really believe in; and the belief in a thing makes it happen. — Frank Lloyd Wright

What you pay attention to expands. Worry makes the concern uppermost in your mind. Compassion keeps your heart open. Fear arouses the defenses of the body. Love relaxes and creates receptivity. What are you paying attention to today?

What general approach do you take to life? Do you believe that most people are well intended? Or, do you think most folks are just waiting for an opportunity to take advantage of you or make you wrong? Do you believe that you deserve love and respect? Or, do you expect to be discounted or overlooked? Do you believe that you can do almost anything you really set your mind to? Or, do you believe that many things are well beyond your reach?

You can choose winning or whining as your basic approach to life. Which do you usually choose?

Is life happening to you or do you make life happen? Do you get up in the morning with a thought of "Good grief! Another day to get through." or "Great! Another day to *give* through!"? You can change your perspective and your perception. That is your choice.

Pay attention to how you want to feel and move towards that. You may have to "Fake it 'til You Make it", but, only a little to get you going. Focus on what you are giving, rather than on what you are not getting. This helps.

Write down the most important belief that you want to live from today. Make it short and memorable, positive and present tense. Remind yourself of it throughout the day. Each time you are put on hold, repeat it to yourself. Each time you are waiting for a light to change, repeat it. Soon it will become a habit of mind and you are on your way!

Caring For Yourself...

When we truly care for ourselves, it becomes possible to care far more profoundly about other people. — Eda LeShan

When I was a child, being thought of as selfish was almost the worst thing that could be said about me! It was designed to instill guilt immediately. Perhaps this happened to you, too.

On reflection, this was an almost crippling blow to self-esteem. No one seemed clear about where self-esteem ended and selfishness began. To be safe, I was carefully schooled to consider that to ask for anything I wanted or needed was an indicator of selfishness. It was also considered rank selfishness to speak well of oneself.

If this was true in your upbringing, I encourage you to think differently now. Celebrate your strengths, talents, skills and accomplishments. It is not conceit to know the good about yourself; however, it is arrogance to suggest that others are inferior. Big difference.

Taking good care of yourself is sometimes strangely linked with selfishness at some deep level within. Folks, then, often neglect themselves in ways that would enhance their self-esteem and improve their health.

Take good care of yourself so that you have the gift of caring to give to others. Remember, you cannot give a gift you do not have.

...Caring For Yourself

For today, find three small ways to take good care of yourself, and DO IT! Make a plan to do something good for yourself every day. You deserve to be taken care of well and you're just the person to do it!

Assume The Best...

Assume that all human beings desire warm, close relationships with each other. — Ricky Sherover-Marcuse

Gandhi said, "We must be the change we would like to see in the world." For quite a while, I have had a vision and a plan for creating a more peaceful world. I'll share it with you, as you might like to join in.

In each of the ten major world spiritual traditions, there is a directive. My rephrasing of it is: Give only what you are willing to receive. You may know it as The Golden Rule. *

My vision is this: If every person in this world who says that they ascribe to one of those spiritual traditions, would agree to practice just this one thing in a focused way for one month, we would have a much more loving and peaceful world. Imagine if every person took it to heart in whatever form he or she found acceptable, from a spiritual point of view or from a "just good common sense" point of view! And if we all did it simultaneously for a month! It would have to have a major impact on our world.

Would you be willing to "Give only what you are willing to receive" for a month, very consciously? It is an amazing exercise in creating quality relationships.

*Do unto others, as you would have them do unto you.

Consider the relationships in your life in which it would be most challenging to "Give only what you are willing to receive".

What would they require of you in order to do this? Are you willing?

Enrich Your World...

You are not here merely to make a living. You are here in order to enable the world to live more amply, with greater vision, with a finer spirit of hope and achievement. You are here to enrich the world and you impoverish yourself if you forget the errand. — Woodrow Wilson

Remembering your definite major purposes in life will save you much time, energy and stress. When you take side roads, tempting as they may be, do it consciously. Those side roads may still get you to your destination. That is not the issue. Taking side roads without consciously choosing to meander is unproductive.

Productivity, in this case, is not about how much you can get done in how short a time frame. Productivity is about you realizing your major goals in life within the time frames *you* have chosen. If you say that you want to write a book, there is only one way to do it. Sit in front of your writing implements, put your hands on the keyboard or pen, and do it! Yes, you can productively spend time gathering facts, statistics, quotes, books, and websites about your topic. Even that has to end… and you have to write!

Whatever your major purposes are, stay on track. Keep moving forward. Make weekly goals, small steps, and complete them. Break the major task into tiny pieces, do one tiny piece and you have accomplished something.

The reward for staying on the path you've chosen is a sense of peace, well-being and accomplishment. If this sounds enticing, you can create it for yourself.

Think about yesterday. How much time did you spend accomplishing a step toward a major goal? If one of your goals is to live a balanced life, did you spend some time relaxing away from any concerns with career? If your goal is to be healthier, did you carefully choose what you ate? What things could you do a little better with today?

Self-Confidence...

Confidence comes not from always being right but from not fearing to be wrong. — Peter T. McIntyre.

How do you build unstoppable self-confidence? If you know how, have you done it? If you've done it, do you maintain it? If you wish you had it, how far do you think you are from it?

Unstoppable self-confidence comes from keeping agreements. In particular, keeping agreements you make with yourself. Do you do what you say you'll do for yourself? Do you do what you say you'll do for others?

Are you your own best friend? How would you feel if your best friend promised to do something important for you but found it more enjoyable to lie on the couch and forget to do it? You get the point!

Unstoppable self-confidence comes from keeping your agreements AND believing that you have something to offer to the world. If you are capable of sitting up and taking nourishment, you have something of value to offer to the world.

What have you been promising to do for yourself? It may even be the same thing you write for your New Year's Resolutions each year.

Think of the most important gift you could give yourself. What stops you from doing this? Most likely, it is not something that requires much money. Often it requires time, solitude, willingness, motivation, or self-respect.

Make a plan to give yourself this one thing.

Let nothing stop you.

Master One Thing...

If one is master of one thing and understands one thing well, one has at the same time, insight into and understanding of many things.
— Vincent Van Gogh

What have you mastered in your life? It may have begun with tying your shoelaces and gone on to many other things since then.

Some things folks master are useful and motivating; others may be negative and impeding. You may have mastered the art of conversation. Extremely useful. You may have mastered the art of procrastination. Not so useful!

Anything that has become a habit is quite likely to be something that you've mastered. Now is a good time to take stock of these things. Are they working to your advantage or are they working against you? Is there something that you would like to master that would serve you better? For most folks, there is.

Spend some time thinking about your 'masterpieces*'. Would you like them to be what you're known for? The good news is that you created them. You are powerful and can create new ones at any time. What will you create today?

* You'll find new ideas and direction in Dr. Shaler's audio tape, 'You are the Mastermind of Your Masterpiece', and other motivating tapes. See the complete list at the back of this book!

Learning...

Aim for success, not perfection. Never give up your right to be wrong, because then you will lose the ability to learn new things and to move forward with your life. — Dr. David Burns

Many people do not seem to know that mistakes are for learning. When you choose a course of action— even just which restaurant to eat in—you create the climate for learning. It may be a mistake, or a delicious discovery. The learning will be in the experience.

Most decisions are not life or death decisions. Those are rare. Yet, it is not uncommon for people to create a great deal of anxiety and angst when faced with a decision. Napoleon Hill suggests that there is wisdom in not trusting a person who has all the facts and still refuses to make a decision. You decide!

So, what if you are wrong? The most simplistic answer to that is that you then have the opportunity to decide again.

Somewhere in our convoluted culture, there is a great fear of "being wrong". Make decisions boldly. You will move forward more quickly. Taking action on sufficient information leads to learning. If it turns out to be a mistake, you've learned something. If it turns out to be just the right thing, you've learned something. Very seldom will the answer to the question, "What if I'm wrong?" have dire consequences. If you need reassurance, ask yourself that question followed by "What is the worst thing that could happen if I AM wrong?" If you could live with that, move boldly forward.

Ask yourself if there is any decision in your life that you are putting off.
Is there a goal you are not moving toward?

Reflect on the reasons you give yourself for doing that.
What is the worst thing that could happen if you proceeded to make the decision and you were wrong?
What is the best thing that could happen if you were right?

Weigh your answers, and proceed.

What You Think...

The happiness of your life depends upon the quality of your thoughts.
— Marcus Aurelius

Have you ever wanted something in your life to be completely, fully, and singularly within your control? You've got it! You have the opportunity to completely control what you think. The brain is a simple binary machine. It can only think about one thing at one time, even though it can do that very quickly. With practice, you can decide exactly what you want to pay attention to, and eliminate the chatter and racing thoughts—the monkey mind.

You've probably had the experience of having your mind fixate on a negative thought. That's called worrying. Worrying about something that might happen or something that seems out of our control is a poor use of energy. Deciding to pay attention to the positive is a good remedy for that.

If you are having doubts that you can control your thoughts, practice. Sit for a while and pay attention to where your mind wanders. Decide what you want to think about and bring your mind back to it each time it wanders. Choose something simple such as deciding on your favorite vacation spot. Each time the mind wanders to thoughts of money, available time, or anything aside from the vacation, re-focus.

Your thoughts are powerful. And, what you pay attention to expands!

What You Think...

Watch your thoughts. If they slip into the places that use your energy in ways you consider poor, bring them back on track. You do have the ability to control the quality of your thoughts, and, therefore, where they take you. Are you going in the right direction?

A Happy Marriage...

A happy marriage is a long conversation that always seems too short.* — *Andre Maurais

When two people decide to live together, the reasons for doing so had best include a great friendship. I'm sure that you have had the experience of not wanting a conversation to end. Marriage or life-partnership can be that kind of an ongoing conversation. There is always something more to say, another subject to explore, new insights to be gathered. You want to know more and more about the other's thoughts and feelings. You consult him/her to expand your own thinking. You trust your partner to give you reliable feedback. You listen to each other carefully. This is partnership!

Partnership is complementary. There are the commonalities that drew you together and the distinct experiences and learning that each contributes. You know the adage, "None of us is as smart as all of us." That's true in your primary relationship as well. Asking one another for insight, input or advice demonstrates trust and openness. Healthy relationships share this information without attachment to its use! They do not play "I-told-you-so!" games, even when it is tempting to do so. Those games demonstrate one-upmanship rather than partnership.

If you are living with another adult, is he or she your very good friend? Can you trust your partner to be totally kind and totally honest at the same time? I hope so. If so, thank your partner today for being in your life. If not, your relationship might need a tune-up.

Sometimes relationships are taken for granted. Think about all your important relationships. Do these folks know how important they are to you? When was the last time you told them? It might be time to make a few phone calls, write a few letters, or make some time to meet for coffee.
No one is in a relationship with a mind reader!
Tell people they matter to you. Better yet, show them!

What It Takes...

Success is that old ABC: ability, breaks and courage. — Charles Luckman

This quote offers the beginning of a recipe for success, but not the whole recipe. One major missing ingredient is the passion, another, the willingness to stay focused on a definite major purpose in life. There is a certain amount of ability that is required, however, stick-to-it-iveness seems to win the day.

You've probably heard about Thomas Edison who, in varying accounts, is said to have accepted his numerous attempts to create a light bulb as learning experiences, never failures. That is the kind of "sticking to the knitting" that is required. That takes courage AND ability.

Occasionally, very occasionally, breaks just "happen", however, it is far more usual that breaks come as the result of persistently knocking on the doors of opportunity. You've heard of actors who were supposedly discovered and instantly became stars. The truth of that matter is usually that they have been working in the arts for years, waiting on tables, passionately pursuing what they love to do, and, finally, the 'someone of note' noticed. The 'overnight' sensation was fifteen years in the making!

What is your recipe for success? Are you following it?

Find what you have a passion for—you'll know what that is because it makes you want to get up in the morning and get right to it—and pursue it relentlessly. It will get you where you want to go!

Write your passions here and review them often...

Gratitude...

If you haven't all the things you want, be grateful for the things you don't have that you wouldn't want. —Anonymous

There is great wisdom in focusing on what you are grateful for in your life. It is an excellent practice to list these things for yourself just before you go to sleep each night, or on first waking each morning. Remember, your mind uses less energy focusing on positive thoughts than on negative ones! So, being grateful is easier on you than complaining or worrying!

There is a Buddhist saying that suggests that people are happiest when they know what, with dignity, they can live without. There is freedom in that, and, in being clear about what it is you wish to be, do and have in your life.

You need to know both your purpose and your guiding principles. When you walk unfettered by "shoulds", clearly focused on your purpose, you will succeed.

Reflect on your purpose and the guiding principles you have chosen for your life. Work with these concepts in your journal. Clarify them. Make your plans for the next three months.

Set goals for this week and make sure that they are "do-able" with a little stretch.

Negative Influences...

Get all the negative people out of your life. They're their own funeral and you can't allow yourself to be buried with them. — Ray Bradbury

Do YOU generally fall into the category of being a negative person? If that happens to be the case, I'm assuming Ray Bradbury is not suggesting suicide! You do have choice about seeing that cup half empty or half full, and, yes, sometimes the thing just IS half empty. It is how you generally approach life and its opportunities that count.

Fortunately, you are 100% able to take charge of your attitude and make it generally positive. Secondly, you then need to assess those in your life who lift you up and those who tear you down... again generally.

The first group to spend less time with are the most destructive... the ones who cannot or will not see the good in you. Reducing their airtime in your life will make an immediate improvement.

Here's a very important thing to consider: many people are still seeking approval in life from people they don't even approve of. If this is true in any of your relationships, cut the cord!

It is sometimes difficult to move away from some folks. It will take some strong decisions, as well as some strong words, to remove them. You'll need a plan.

I remember when I first realized that my mother was constantly raining on everyone's parade. I made a decision to tell her that I loved her and wanted to spend time with her AND that I would remove my children and myself when she started to "rain". I had to leave several times before she believed me. It was a wonderful gift for us all.

What is your plan to stop the "rain"?

Choose You...

To succeed, one must possess an effective combination of ability, ambition, courage, drive, hard work, integrity and loyalty.
— Harry F. Banks

Some days just getting out of bed, or putting one foot in front of the other, are major achievements, aren't they? Other days, is it as if time was expanded and your interest and energy seem endless? Do you know what makes the difference?

For many people, life is moving so quickly that the time to learn about themselves is eroded. Snatch your life back from the 'busy-ness' monster. Time to remember that you are in charge of your choices. You decide how you fill your time...or if you answer that telephone. Therefore, you decide how tired or energetic you will be. Of course, there are things that take that decision out of your hands. Chronic or acute illness, a broken ankle or unbalanced metabolism can certainly change that equation. Loss of a love, a loved one or a job also can put you on the sidelines temporarily.

Stop, look and listen. Stop for a while. Look at your last seventy-two hours and ask yourself if how you spent it is all right with you. Listen to your body. Ask it if it is feeling taken care of, looked after, and cherished. Find out what it needs right now and make a plan to take care of it.

Spend no time being hard on yourself. Proceed in the direction of your goals. Make choices that honor your goals, your health and your sense of well-being.

Each time you stop for a red light today, ask yourself, "Are there any other red lights in my life that I would be wise to pay attention to?"

Your body may want you to slow down to allow it to catch up.

Calmness...

Silence is a great teacher and to learn its lessons you must pay attention to it. There is no substitute for the creative inspiration, knowledge, and stability that come from knowing how to contact your core of inner silence. The great Sufi poet, Rumi, wrote, "Only let the moving waters calm down, and the sun and moon will be reflected on the surface of your being. — Deepak Chopra

When you take time to sit still and focus quietly on nothing more than creating stillness within, there are great benefits. This world is often focused on "busy-ness" and maintaining that busyness keeps you from knowing yourself well.

Sometimes folks purposefully keep themselves busy in an effort not to think about or confront an issue, a loss, or a decision. You have probably heard that advice—"Just Keep Busy". It can help you avoid thinking and, therefore, avoid pain. On the other hand, it can also help you avoid feeling and this is not always wise.

Spend time sitting quietly each day. There is great pleasure in doing so. Sit upright with both feet on the floor. Take a few deep breaths and release them slowly through your mouth. Focus your mind on a beautiful image or sound. Continue to do this for a few minutes. Hold your mind on the image and relax.

Consciously using your breath to relax is the quickest, easiest and least expensive way to remove tension.

It is useful and self-affirming to spend quiet time with yourself every day. Find a few minutes and make it a sacred time for you. Begin with five minutes. You will likely find it so enjoyable and reap so many benefits that it will soon become twenty!

Impossible To Fail...

All that is necessary to break the spell of inertia and frustration is this: Act as if it were impossible to fail. That is the talisman, the formula, the command of right about face that turns us from failure to success.
— Dorothea Brande

What would you do if you knew you could not fail? That's a great beginning question for finding your passion. Do you know what you would do?

Certainly, it would be unrealistic to think that you might not encounter obstacles. You may find resistances within yourself, too. The courage to act as though you cannot fail will carry you through those if your passion is strong enough. No, it is not just the passion. It is also the persistence, the drive to reach your goal that leads to success. Applying that drive to find ways around obstacles and ways to overcome your own inertia and resistance to change will get results. It will also teach you that you are more powerful than you might have thought.

Some things get stopped right at the idea level. You think, "I'd love to do that." and the Inner Critic says, "Who are you kidding?" First things first: Answer that with "I can do anything I set my mind to doing. Watch me!" It is not just positive thought, though. It requires action—daily, consistent, positive steps. Keep your mind focused on what you wish to accomplish. Do things that take you in that direction. Surround yourself with folks who want you to get there... and do not stop!

For a few minutes today, remember what you most wanted to do when you were young. Have you done it? Does it still light you up? What would you like to do now? Choose something small and accomplish it. This will build your confidence for the larger things.

Look back a few years and make a list of your accomplishments. Spend some time celebrating all that you have done. You are successful in so many ways. Now, what is your next success?

Evading Your Possibilities...

If you deliberately plan to be less than you are capable of being, then I warn you that you will be unhappy for the rest of your lives. You'll be evading your own capacities, your own possibilities. — Abraham Maslow

The word of great interest in this quote is "deliberately". The dictionary says it means "characterized by or resulting from careful and thorough consideration and characterized by awareness of the consequences". Are you being deliberate when you choose what to do with your time and money?

These are the two areas that will demonstrate what you are actually currently valuing. How you spend your time and how you spend your money are good indicators of what is important to you.

When you consider your use of time and money, do your uses reflect what you say is most important to you?

Evading Your Possibilities...

Do a quick audit of your checkbook and calendar for last week. Do they reflect your stated priorities in life? If so, celebrate. If not, is it time for a change?

Unrelenting Determination...

Commitment is an unrelenting determination to achieve your goals. If commitment is to exist, it is created through courage, tenacity and the willingness to feel the fear of the past and not allow it to create your future. Commitment is truly a road besieged by unknown obstacles and arduous climbs. It is only through commitment that possibilities become achievements and dreams become realities. — Author Unknown. Quote in Steve Shulls, Performance Coaching Newsletter

Commitment is a word that is reported to intimidate the unattached! Usually, that refers to long-time singles, however, think about it in a new way. Commitment is the very opposite of unattached in reference to your vision and your goals as well. Let's not use the word lightly. To make a commitment is a serious undertaking.

Are you wishing you could have the life you say you want, or, are you committed to creating it? Big difference. Being committed requires you to have your ducks in a row and keep them there. You set your compass and stay on course.

Do you know the things, events, people or situations that are most likely to distract you from your path? So many people are so good at creating distractions, procrastinations, reasons and excuses, and making them sound logical! Sure, there are sometimes things that unexpectedly intervene, but most things are completely within your control. If the event itself is beyond your control, your response to it is not. What are you truly committed to?

...Unrelenting Determination

Make a list of plans, ideas, beliefs and relationships to which you are truly committed. Review each one and reflect on your level of commitment as demonstrated by the time, energy, and resources you devote to it.
Sit with these ideas long enough to get to the deep feeling level.
That is passion. It is either there or not! This is valuable information for you.

Love has nothing to do with what you are expecting to get, only with what you are expecting to give... which is everything. — Katherine Hepburn

There are many suggestions for how to get what you want in this world. One I really like is "you'll get what you want when you help those around you get what they want". Everybody wins! This creates a great sense of connectedness and, therefore, community. Everyone has the opportunity to be loving, thoughtful, caring and respectful...and get what he or she wants, too.

In business, this is called the referral process. Outside of business, it's called friendship. How are you helping your friends and colleagues get what they want? What more could you do for them? Have you discussed with them what it is they want? If you are both clear about what you each want, it will make it much easier to create plans to achieve your goals.

Do you usually work with others or are you a lone ranger? Think of inviting a friend or colleague to join with you in a strategic alliance to assist each of you to reach your goals. You might even like to invite one or two others and achieve exponentially.

Consider asking someone to join with you to achieve a particular goal. Find out what you can do for them, too. Make a plan to check in with each other regularly to share your progress on each other's behalf as well as your own. Celebrate heartily.

Be Careful...

Before strongly desiring anything, we should look carefully into the happiness of its present owner. — Francois De La Rochefoucauld

Be careful what you wish for. A full investigation is in order. If you truly believe you want something, take the time to look into the realities of having it. What would change in your life?

Most folks wish for a large windfall of money. Their thoughts are around what that money would buy for them including time and freedom. Do they think about the changes that money would bring? About people perceiving them differently? About people having expectations of them? About boredom setting in when there is no longer work to be done? About living after the excitement, after the 'splash' of winning?

Statistics show that most people who win large amounts of money are worse off two years later than they were prior to winning the money...and their relationships have suffered.

When you think your goals through to the changes their achievement will make in every area of your life, you have a better chance of being pleased with the result. Be careful what you wish for. You may get it and not want it!

Visualize yourself having accomplished your goals. How do you feel? How has life changed? Are all the changes positive? Is it the result you thought it would be? If so, terrific! If not, what can you learn from this exercise. Modify your goal or change it altogether. Goals are meant to improve your life after all.

(By the way, any goal that fits into the 'should' department 'should' be struck from your list.)

I will not let anyone walk through my mind with their dirty feet.
— Mahatma Gandhi

What would happen if a friend came to visit you and brought a large brown bag of dripping garbage along? Would you let the friend and the garbage into your house? What would happen if you did let the friend and the garbage in and, then, that friend picked up that bag and emptied it on your head? What would you do? What would you say?

You often have conversations with others that are very similar to having someone's dripping garbage poured over you, don't you? Some people are chronic complainers, some incessant whiners, some are filled with anger, and some make a lifestyle of negativity. These are all forms of "dripping garbage".

There are many ways to let someone know your boundaries. If your boundaries exclude being "dumped on", be sure to tell your friends, or relatives. Use language that speaks about yourself and refrains from using the word "you". This helps the other person to hear you.

If folks continue to overstep your boundaries, move away from them. Send clear messages. Be sure to be respectful of others, too. Your behavior always speaks louder than your words.

Think about sending messages to folks in your life who want to walk through your mind with their dirty feet.

Tell them what is important to you and how you want to be treated.
Who do you need to speak to about this soon?

Be The Yeast...

I am personally convinced that one person can be a change catalyst, a "transformer" in any situation, any organization. Such an individual is yeast that can leaven an entire loaf. It requires vision, initiative, patience, respect, persistence, courage and faith to be a transforming leader.
— Stephen R. Covey

A leader is not necessarily the boss, the president or the manager. A leader is any person who chooses to exert influence at any time. That is you! No matter what you are doing, you are exerting influence. You choose whether that influence is negative, positive or, even, indifferent. Leadership in a relationship of any kind is a choice.

You have the opportunity to act as yeast in any situation. You decide what and how you will contribute to any relationship. There are sometimes folks who seem to like to make things difficult. They know everything and insist that their way is the best. Sometimes these folks are insensitive or behaving from sheer insecurity. How can you be a leader in this instance? Good communication skills will help. Acknowledging the contribution and expertise of the "controller" is a beginning. Another useful skill is redirection. Thank them for their contribution and say that you would like to hear from or ask others their opinions so that the group can make a democratic decision.

Yeast makes things rise but it can also just make things bigger. In any situation you have the opportunity to raise the communication and relationship to a higher level, or just augment the problem. Which will you choose?

When you encounter a person who is being difficult, take a deep breath and consider that that person may simply need recognition. In an honest and caring way, find something that you like about them or about their position and mention it. Sometimes that is difficult.
That is probably a very good time to say, "You could be right!"
That statement, followed by active listening, is very powerful!

No Whining...

While others may argue about whether the world ends with a bang or a whimper. I just want to make sure mine doesn't end with a whine.
— Barbara Gordon

Have you ever noticed how attractive whining is? The word, "attract", means to pull or draw something towards you. Can whining draw people and change to you? Probably not. Yet, it is a vastly over-employed approach. Being able to attract to you what you want to create in life means firing the whining approach.

Imagine a day without whining—without anyone whining. Wouldn't that be delightful? No one moaning and dripping about what they do not have; No one complaining about things rather than taking steps to change them. They may even just take the weather in their stride. This approach would brighten everyone's day!

Listen to yourself. If you hear a whine creeping in, simply stop in mid-sentence and say, "Let me re-phrase that." Change your message to state what it is that you would like to have happen and add a few words about what you are going to do to make it happen. You'll soon find that things are going better for you. If someone else's whining is within earshot, simply say, "Let's think in positive terms. What would you like to have happen?" You can, of course, go on and ask them what they are willing to do to bring it about. No guarantees that the whining will stop. After all, some people make it a lifestyle. You can do your part, though, in changing yourself and your approach...and, if necessary, your environment!

Think about the folks in your life who whine. What is its effect on you? How does it affect the way you feel about them? You may notice that these folks diminish your energy and that they may even feel "toxic" to you. Make a plan to address the issue with them as suggested above. Sometimes you may have to be quite forthright. It's worth it!

Good Thoughts...

Every good thought you think is contributing its share to the ultimate result of your life. — Grenville Kleiser

What would it take to change your life just 1% today? Let's say that you are awake for sixteen hours a day. Sixteen hours are nine hundred and sixty minutes. One per cent of that is a mere 9.6 minutes. You could begin by doing something good for yourself, something clearly contributing to reaching your goals for an extra 9.6 minutes a day. Of course, that is not improving your life one- percent but it is a good beginning. You would have to determine what the one per cent solution for you would look and feel like, but it would not take very much.

The real trick is in sustaining the changes! It will take a strong will and a consistent, conscious decision. The truth is that even if you decided to improve your life one-half of one per cent a day, every day, you would still be way ahead!

Remember the safety lecture you get each time you begin a flight. Be sure you know where the exits are.... and the closest one may be behind you. The same is true with making positive changes. You may think that you do not have time to add another thing, and not realize that the best change might be to stop doing something!

No matter how the world conspires, you are the one who chooses how you spend your time.

Set aside twenty minutes or so to reflect on how you spent each hour of the day yesterday. What would you have done differently if you had the perfect life?

Intimacy...

As long as we are looking outside ourselves for intimacy, we will never have it and we will never be able to share it. In order to be intimate with another person, we have to know who we are, what we feel, what we think, what our values are, what is important to us, and what we want. If we do not know these things about ourselves, we can never share them with another person. — Anne Wilson Schaef

How well do you know yourself? When you look at something, can you immediately tell if you like it? When you are invited somewhere, do you know if you want to go? When it is mealtime, do you know what you want to eat?

If you were asked to list the three things that you value most, could you? Do you know what really pleases you? If someone said they would like to do something really nice for you, do you know what you would want?

You've likely heard that you can achieve what you can conceive and believe. A Harvard study following the lives of a graduating class over twenty years found that the most successful graduates, and yes, the wealthiest too, were the ones who had written and reviewed their goals and pursued them with passion. The clarity they had about what they wanted in their lives translated into action and they met or exceeded their goals consistently.

Making a "dream inventory". List all the things you would like to be, do and have before you are finished with living... no restrictions, no limitations. Keep the list in a visible place and feel free to add to it. There will be something on your list that you can do today.

Do it! Enjoy!

Step Out...

Twenty years from now you will be more disappointed by the things you didn't do than by the ones you did do. So throw off the bowlines. Sail away from the safe harbor. Catch the trade winds in your sails. Explore. Dream. Discover. — Mark Twain

Have you ever given yourself one of these reasons why you could not follow your dream? It's (a) not a good time, (b) a silly idea, (c) too risky, (d) not guaranteed to succeed, (e) too expensive, (f) too disruptive to the flow of life? Or, "I'm (a) too old, (b) too young, (c) too poor, (d) too inexperienced, thin, fat…"? How do you feel about that "road not taken" now? What would have happened if you had followed your heart or your dream? Where would you be today? What would be different?

Live fully. Embrace change. Follow your passion and inspiration…and see where it leads. Use your intelligence and common sense, of course.

There are too many people who have regretted decisions to stick with the status quo when their hearts wanted to soar. Look at what holds you in one place or why you may have decided to tread water. If it is dampening your spirit on a regular basis, get in the flow and swim! At the least, you'll get exercise. At the most, you'll arrive somewhere new and interesting…. perhaps the place of your dreams!

...Step Out

Do you have a long-time secret desire? Is there something you would fill in this blank with, "Life would be perfect is only I could_________"

Write three steps you could take right away to move in the direction of the goal.

That's how dreams are realized.

Class is an aura of confidence. That is sure without being cocky. Class has nothing to do with money. Class never runs scared. It is self-discipline and self-knowledge. It's the sure-footedness that comes with having proved you can meet life. — Ann Landers

How confident do you feel? Can you walk into any room feeling that you are lovable, acceptable and deserving of approval? Do your posture, eye contact and presence convey that message? Every person brings a gift to the world. The question is only: Are you going to open it?

What if you saw your birthday in a new way? Not from the "Oh, another year gone, another year older. Oh, dear!" perspective, but rather from "This is the anniversary of the day I graced the world with my presence!" You were born with wonderful abilities. You can light up a life and a room. First you have to turn on your own light, though.

Here's a daily exercise to help you shine brighter! Each morning, before you clean your teeth or comb your hair, go directly to the bathroom mirror. Look deeply into your eyes and hold your gaze. Then, out loud, say to yourself: "*I love you. I accept you. I approve of you just the way you are*!" and throw yourself a big kiss. Do it ever morning without fail for a month. Does that sound wild?

Give the gift you are today. Be present, available, and confident that you can make a difference. Remember the words of Igor Silorsky: "The work of the individual still remains the spark that moves mankind forward." Be that spark!

Make a list of all the things you have to give to the world—all the good things about you. Read it several times and continue to add to it forever. You have so much good in you and so much to give.

Trust Yourself...

As soon as you trust yourself, you will know how to live. — Goethe

Do you listen to your body? Do you listen when you have a reaction to something or someone and you just "know something is amiss? Whether you call it intuition or inner knowing, it is your senses rallying to give you good information. You meet a new person and you instantly feel comfortable with him or her. Or, you may instantly feel cautious.

Trusting yourself to know what is best is important. You can always get more information if you need it. Sometimes you have trained yourself to overlook or ignore what you really "know" to be true for yourself. Sometimes, too, you have learned to talk yourself out of your "knowing" by over-ruling it with your "shoulds", "ought-tos" and "have-tos".

It is wise to listen to your body. Those clues contain valuable information.

Think about times you have and have not listened.
Which works better for you?

Living Your Passion...

Throw your heart over the fence and the rest will follow.
— Norman Vincent Peale

Aside from the Nike slogan, "Just Do It"®, this quote may be the next shortest reminder to live your passion. Often in workshops and seminars, people tell me that they don't know what they are passionate about. In fact, some people are still wondering what truly brings them joy.

You may know what brings you pleasure but not what truly gives you that feeling that "Yes, THIS is what I'm supposed to be doing with my life!" It is very difficult to find this if you are filled with stress and tension. It is difficult even to laugh honestly and heartily when constant tension makes it so that laughing turns immediately to tears…tears of tension release rather than hilarity.

Do you know what you like, appreciate, or are interested in? Not those tension-filled, looking for approval, trying to "do it right", be a great parent-employee-entrepreneur-community worker-chauffeur-nurse-caretaker-nurturer-partner-musician-writer-and-more based choices. Those are more likely to be expectations firmly implanted by society rather than passions. Do you know what your conscious choices are?

Know what lights you up, what lifts your spirits and raises your sights. Know what makes you say 'YES!" inside and find a way to express it in your daily life.

® Registered Trademark of the Nike Corporation

Spend some time today thinking about what really brings you joy, what makes your heart sing, and what makes it possible for you to smile from the inside out. Then you'll be on the path to living your passion.

Questioning...

The important thing is to not stop questioning. — Albert Einstein

Have you ever heard someone say, "I'll just have to accept my fate."? Did you find it an empowering thing to hear? It could mean that the person believes they have done everything in their power to bring about the outcome they desire. Then, they are willing to accept their fate. On the other extreme, it could mean, "I have no control at all. I'll have to take what life hands out to me." It is the latter that saddens me. How about you?

We all ask ourselves a lot of questions, don't we? What is the quality of the questions you ask yourself? Do you say things like, "Why me? Why does this always happen to me?" or "Why did she say that?" or "What did I do wrong?" These are not high-quality questions.

High-quality questions move you forward immediately. They focus on positive direction and indicate an understanding of what's possible. Here are a few: "How can I turn this around?" or "How can I make it work?", "How can I utilize this?" or "How can I use this to empower myself and others?" The answers to these questions increase your personal power and your power to change the world around you.

The quality of your life can relate directly to the quality of the questions you ask yourself.

Keep a small book handy and make a note of the typical questions you ask yourself during the day. Do they move you forward or do they reinforce your sense of powerlessness? When a question shows up in your head, deliberately re-state it as a high-quality question.
This habit will change your view of life quickly.

An Educated Person...

An educated person is one who has developed the faculties of his mind such that he can get what he wants without it costing another.
— Napoleon Hill

"Win-win" solutions are generally the most profitable. They not only give each party something they each want, they also preserve and enhance the relationships and move them forward. Learning to create "win-win" solutions is worth the effort. It takes both willingness and ability.

When you use your mind to set clear intentions you subconsciously begin to create the circumstances to achieve your goals. Even before you begin to actively work on objectives and tasks, holding that clear intention in your mind starts the process. The mind is powerful!

Did you know that psycholinguistic research tells us that it takes the mind 48% longer to understand a negative statement than a positive one? It would seem to make sense, then, to keep in mind the things you want, the things you are moving toward.

Many folks concentrate on what they are avoiding, the things they definitely do not want. Clearly, this research tells us why that is so much work! It also tells us why a compliment works much better than a criticism. Go for the positive!

Are you sending yourself more negative messages than positive ones?
How do you speak to and about yourself in your mind?

Try this:
Only say things about yourself that you want to be true...
even the things you say in your head!

Security...

There is no security on this earth, there is only opportunity.
— General Douglas MacArthur

The era known as the "Great Depression" left seemingly indelible marks on the Baby Boomers of North American culture. Fortunately, as with most things, the mark is fading as new generations and new economic conditions prevail. That mark was a strong ethic to create security.

My generation, trained by those who both experienced the Depression in their formative years and were raised by Victorians, were taught by both example and experience to hang on to what they had because they might need it! This may be one of the major reasons we have so much clutter in our lives. Those possessions, jobs, and relationships supposedly represented "security".

Security is found in your mind—information and skills you have acquired, experiences you have learned from, where you focus your attention. Where do you think your security lies?

If you accept the idea that security—aside from the financial security of a few million dollars in gold buried in an earthquake free area, carefully marked and known only to you—is found within yourself, then you walk in the world in a different way. You can see opportunities more clearly, accept challenges, and even risks, more readily, and worry far, far less. You are equipped with all that you need to be secure at all times.

Spend a few minutes reflecting on where you believe your security lies. Follow those thoughts through to the feelings attached to them. Where did you make these decisions? Would you like to choose differently...or are you secure?

Making A Life...

We make a living by what we get, but we make a life by what we give.
— Winston Churchill

How are you making a contribution to life? When I used to work extensively with folks with life-threatening diagnoses, one of the pieces of the healing puzzle for them was to find a place to volunteer and help others. Why? Because giving of their time, energy and skills helped them to focus outwardly. When we are focused on giving, magic happens.

Explore the phrase, "You get what you want by helping others get what they want". Do you believe it?

Is there someone you could help today? Perhaps your life partner? Someone who is struggling to accomplish something? Find someone today and give him or her some of your time. You'll quickly understand how to make this magic happen.

You have likely been moved by some need in the world. Aside from the feeling that something needs to be done, what action do you take? Your willingness to send a note, give money, spend time or offer your services brings about change in this world.

Giving opens your heart. Decide where to give today.

Superior to Circumstance...

Nothing splendid has ever been achieved except by those who dared believe that something inside them was superior to circumstance.
— Bruce Barton

Do you feel superior to circumstance? Do you feel confident that you can manage most things that come your way? You can, of course, if you believe you can. Yes, that can sound too easy. You may find yourself saying, "Yes, but, if you only knew what I have to contend with...". You do have the ultimate control over your response to circumstances, don't you?

If you believe you have choice in the ways that you respond to whatever is next in your life, you are well on your way. If you can suspend judging circumstances as good or bad, right or wrong, and just consider them as "next", you will have more energy to meet the challenge.

Much energy is lost bemoaning situations, rather than getting on with solutions. Think of an office when something goes wrong. How much time is spent over coffee and lunch debriefing the "problem" and airing grievances? Yes, acknowledging feelings is important and necessary, however, once...and I mean once... that is well done, it is time to go to solution. Be forward thinking. Move forward. Take action.

...Superior to Circumstance

What is your pattern when circumstances challenge you? When folks live with "Ain't it awful?" and "They done me wrong." attitudes and spend their time garnering support for their problem, they seldom feel good.

Do you acknowledge your feelings, round up your resources and move forward? That is a very good way to eliminate energy leaks and build self-esteem.

Being Ashamed...

Live never to be ashamed if anything you do or say is published around the world—even if what is published is not true. — Richard Bach

Isn't it true that you have absolutely no control over how another person interprets your words and actions? Whether you speak or are silent, whether you attend or are absent, a message is sent. The receiver of that message does with it what they want. Wow, putting it that way, it's amazing people get up in the morning! You must be very brave!

You are also very skilled. You may have already learned a very important secret. That secret is the knowledge that, to build a trusting relationship, you have to understand one another's expectations. When you understand that, you improve the chances of being interpreted correctly. The trick, though, is to spend enough time exploring those expectations —understanding the needs, wants, fear, desires, insecurities, skills of another person AND being honest in the process. Once you have shared these things you have taken much of the guesswork out of the relationship. Without this knowledge, working or living together is somewhat akin to a walk in a minefield!

Examine your relationships. Do you know the expectations? Have you openly discussed what you are willing and capable of bringing to the relationship? Have you clearly delineated your boundaries? Doing these things will bring much richness to your relationships as well as reducing tension.

A Good Idea...

Get a good idea and stick with it. Dog it, and work at it until it's done and done right. — Walt Disney

One of the great challenges in life is to stay focused and not to go madly off in all directions. It makes so much sense, doesn't it? How is it, then, that most people do not find it easy to stay on track with their goals? After all, they chose their goals, so they must be appealing!

Is it difficult for you to stay focused on your goals? How much prompting does it take for you to abandon what you are doing and do something else? What is it about that "something else" that is so appealing? What is it about your goal that is not appealing enough, perhaps? Big questions.

Avoidance can be a big issue. Often you call it procrastination, however, it really is avoidance. When there is a task to do, do you often find yourself deciding to clean your desk, make unnecessary phone calls, or, even counting all the staples in that little box just to be sure there really are 1,000.

Take stock when this happens! You want to do things you love to do. You'll even do some very unpleasant things to achieve a desired result...if this were not true, who would undergo cosmetic dentistry or liposuction? If you are focused on what you REALLY want, you may have to remind yourself that the task that seems unappealing is really your ticket to your dreams. Pay for it!

Reaffirm your goals. Make sure they truly reflect what you want. Sit with each of your goals—read it out loud, close your eyes, see how your body reacts to each.

Goals that truly light you up and/or contribute to your sense of well-being and peace are the ones to focus on.
Keep the others for another time...or release them completely.

The quality of a person's life is in direct proportion to their commitment to excellence, regardless of their chosen endeavor. — Vince Lombardi

Many of us have often heard the phrase, "If it's worth doing, it's worth doing well". I know it echoed through my childhood. I think it prevented me from dabbling in things for the sheer pleasure of experiencing them or, perhaps, for the opportunity to discover a new source of pleasure, to develop a new skill or to find something I never need to do again!

In 1981, I was attending a conference in LA called the Brain-Mind Revolution. Marilyn Ferguson was one of the speakers and she said something that made a lot more sense to me. She questioned, "Surely if a thing is truly worth doing, it must be worth doing even half-___ed?" That seems to be a much more discovery-oriented approach.

Fortunately, everyone does not enjoy the same things. Surely there is wisdom in experiencing things to find out which ones bring you joy. And then, when you have found them, apply Lombardi's quote vigorously.

Give something new a shot. It may be as tiny as driving to work a new way or as huge as going skydiving. Commit to doing something new!

What Are You Looking For?

A pessimist sees the difficulty in every opportunity, an optimist sees the opportunity in every difficulty. — Winston Churchill

Have you ever thought about how you choose to perceive the world? Or even *that* how you perceive the world is a choice? You have the choice in this world to react or respond. Which do you prefer?

Until you understand that both your perceptions and responses are entirely within your control, you may simply react to life…often in a knee-jerk, "Oops!" fashion. You know those because you often find yourself apologizing for them a little later when you wake up!

There is a book that I have found very helpful in life that has as one of its lessons, "Everything has the meaning that I give it". I find that to be both basic and profound. Nothing has meaning in and of itself. It has meaning only when I give it meaning… and then it has the particular meaning that I give it… my own spin! You've had situations in which you perceived the same situation very differently from another person. You remember things differently even when you've seen the same thing. So it is with your view of the world. You choose it- and then it affects everything you experience.

What Are You Looking For?

Before deciding on the meaning of something, see how many possible meanings it could have. Exercise your perception! It could be quite informative.

Living Fully...

Life is a great big canvas, throw all the paint you can at it. — Danny Kaye

What a wonderful idea…throw all the paint you can at it. I wonder if you are very cautious with your "paint". I wonder if you are even cautious with your throwing! I have a guess that there are more small, paint-saving, precise bland drawings that there are big splashes of bold color on most life canvases. What do you think?

Many people are very careful not to make mistakes. They don't seem to believe that mistakes are for learning. The difficulty is not in making a mistake, but in not learning from it…and, then, making it again and again. If you're going to throw paint, you may miss the canvas every once and a while and have to clean up a bit of a mess, however, that seems so much healthier than always holding onto your paint for a "rainy day", to mix metaphors. What if you make a mistake? What if you waste some paint? What if everyone doesn't like your painting? What if you use up all of one color?

There is also another approach that often seems to be practiced. That's the approach of keeping your colors, and criticizing others who are bold enough to paint! Or another, seeing the world as only black and white, and missing the colors altogether.

The joy surely is in the painting.

I bet there is something that you've always wanted to do but held back from doing it. How about doing it, or making a plan to do it...today?

Today's A New Day...

Never let yesterday use up today. — Richard H. Nelson

Do you give yourself a fresh start each morning? That's what each morning really is, right? You have the opportunity to begin again. You might remember what Henry Ford said that even failure "is only the opportunity more intelligently to begin again." What you bring to today from yesterday is entirely your choice.

In fact, the truth is that you have the opportunity to begin again every minute. It's often been a mystery to me why folks go off their diets and have to wait until Monday to begin again! Why not begin again with the next mouthful? If you haven't exercised for three days, why not do it today?

Stay up-to-the-minute with yourself. You're in charge. Begin again more intelligently right this minute!

Could you change your thinking about yourself and your goals? Sure, you could. When it occurs to you that you are off track, get right back on track. Spend no time beating yourself up or making excuses. Simply, begin again more intelligently. You can do this!

Moving Forward...

A new life begins for us with every second. Let us go forward joyously to meet it. We must press on, whether we will or no, and we will walk better with our eyes before us than with them ever cast behind.
— Jerome K. Jerome

Every day you have the opportunity to do things differently. Every day you have the opportunity to change and grow. It is comforting to know that you can reorient yourself in the direction of your goals instantly by reading them and recommitting, sometimes more than once a day!

Some folks "beat themselves up" for mistakes from the past. You know, the "I-should-have-known-better", "I-should-have-seen-it-coming" variety of self-talk. That kind of talk is only useful once or twice in any situation. It only has value if it is used to learn from the experience. Some folks make a life work of beating themselves up for past mistakes, or missed opportunities. In some cultures, people focus entirely on the wrongs done to them generations before and generate anger that prevents them from seeing clearly in the present moment. Energy use is a choice, too.

Knowing both the direction in which you wish your life to go and how you would like to feel on the journey gives you the information necessary for drawing your personal map. Sure, you may find some bridges washed out and have to find alternative pathways. You may find unexpected jungles that slow you down. Remember where you're headed and why and proceed.

Read your goals. (If you do not have any written goals, commit to writing one in each of four categories, today—physical, intellectual, social/emotional and spiritual.) Take one step, large or small, in the direction of at least one goal before you sleep tonight.

Just before you drift off to sleep review your day and acknowledge yourself for the steps you have taken and make a plan for tomorrow.

Shortness of Time...

Those who make the worst use of their time are the first to complain of its shortness. — Jean de la Bruysre

Time is such a precious commodity, isn't it? You hear people talk about there not being enough of it so often.

Recently a colleague of mine told a story about her mentally challenged son, now an adult, who came to her with exciting news. He had heard her say so often that she did not have enough time. Watching TV, he had learned something that he just knew would help his mom. He was watching an ad for cell phones. His excitement came as he told his mom that he could help her because the ad said she could purchase all the extra minutes that she needed from the cell phone company! Many of us wish that that were true, right?

The time you save by planning the way you will use your time will come back to you many times over. When you take the time to take care of your body, mind and spirit, you actually gain time for all those things you want to do.

If you are unsure that this is true, try it for twenty-one days. Set aside 15 or 20 minutes to meditate, clear your mind, read something inspirational, deep breathe, or pray and another 15 or 20 minutes for exercise...even a good brisk walk. Now see how much you gain in terms of energy, clarity, needing less sleep, refreshment. Try it!

Open your mind to the possibility that taking care of yourself pays dividends in time for your worthwhile pursuits. Begin with a fifteen-minute walk. Feel yourself connected to the beauty of nature—remember you are a part of its beauty every minute.

Thinking Makes It So...

You are NOT what you think you are. But what you think—YOU ARE!
— Norman Vincent Peale

If you were to sit down and write a list of words that describe you, would the first things jumping to mind be negatives or positives? I hope they would be positives. The self-talk you engage in has a direct effect on the way you present yourself to the world as well as on how you feel about yourself.

When you enter a room full of folks, think, "I have something of value to offer each person here". As you look at each person in your day, think "I am giving you my best every moment because I care about you and about myself".

I love what Mark Victor Hansen says, too: "When someone tells you "No", think "Next!" It is useful to remember this. It keeps you moving forward rather than stopping in your tracks because one person is not ready for your idea.

When you think about yourself, think positively. When you speak about yourself, speak positively. My friend, Audrey, shared this with me: Never say a word about yourself that you would not want to be true! I love that! It keeps me mindful. Maybe you would like to adopt it, too.

You probably know this: "You're not who you think you are. You're not who other people think you are. You're who you think other people think you are." Well, if it is true, be who you want other people to think you are!

Spend a few quiet minutes today writing a list of all the wonderful, positive things about you.

Focus on these. Feel free to add to the list at any time. Walk right into those good things and wear them well!

Humor is an affirmation of dignity, a declaration of man's superiority to all that befalls him. — Roman Gary

Has humor saved an awkward moment? Has humor saved a relationship? You have probably said or done something... maybe, even, just once...that you really wished you had not done or said. Just when the words were leaving your lips you really, really wanted them back, right? You steeled yourself for the backlash, imagining days of difficulties to follow. Your partner looked at you, made a humorous remark and there was no problem. Wasn't that a relief?

You can be the person who brings humor to a situation. You can be the person who creates that sense of relief for others. Of course, humor has its place. Folks do use it to cover up their feelings, their sensitivities and their inability or unwillingness to address another's concerns. Those issues need attention, too. Humor is not a panacea for relationships. It is simply one tool that can avert unnecessary pain. It can lift pain, too.

Take yourself less seriously. Make light of things that really don't matter. Life goes better when you do. What does it cost you to see the funny side of things? Absolutely nothing. Few things in life are cheaper!

Could you take your life a little less seriously? Could you possibly imagine that people say things that they wished they hadn't, and did not mean—sometimes? You decide when to make light of things and when to delve deeply into the underlying messages. When folks are harried, they are likely to speak without thinking. Give them a break. Let them off the hook if it really doesn't matter. Remember, it's your choice.

What's Needed?

Efforts and courage are not enough without purpose and direction.
— John F. Kennedy

When it's vacation time, you likely travel with airline tickets, a road map or both. You may have accommodation reserved. You know where you are going, or what you want to do. You are aware of the weather, the necessary clothes, equipment, and luggage. Some of you will have even counted the right number of vitamins and supplements for the time you'll be away. Most people spend more time planning for their two or three week vacations, than they do for the remaining weeks of the year. Startling when you think of it that way, isn't it?

People who truly care about themselves care about the way they use their time, energy and resources. They make very conscious choices every day. They plan carefully and execute their plans with the same attention they give their vacations. They know where they are going. They foresee obstacles and overcome them directly. They take full responsibility for their lives. They are accountable.

If you do not know where you want to end up, any path will take you there. Successful people live with intention and focus. Be successful!

What's Needed?

Have you clearly defined your next three goals? Write them here. Can you foresee any likely obstacles? What do you need to do to avoid them? Conserve your resources. Plan wisely.

Rekindling...

In everyone's life at some time our inner fire goes out. It is then burst into flame by an encounter with another human being. We should all be thankful for those people who rekindle the inner spirit.
— Albert Schweitzer

Do you remember the last time you may have felt as though you "just didn't have what it took" or "couldn't get going" anymore? How did you lift yourself out of those doldrums? Who or what was the wind beneath your sails?

It may well have been the words or kindness of another person that provided your "lift". Whether it was reading and being reminded of what is possible, or turning to a friend or mentor for guidance or assistance, your willingness to reach out for inspiration speeded up the process. Knowing your sources of "lift" allows you to quickly get on your path again.

Remember, too, that you have the power to provide "lift" for others. Look for opportunities to do so. It's an upper!

Identify three people (writers included) and three activities that lift you.

When you know how to get yourself out of unproductive valleys, you are more likely to risk with confidence. Be prepared to soar.

Defining Yourself...

Never be bullied into silence. Never allow yourself to be made a victim. Accept no one's definition of your life: define yourself. — Harvey Fierstein

Have you ever come away from a conversation or a meeting wishing that you had spoken your mind, or, at least, asked more questions? Examining the reasons why this happens is important. Sometimes, of course, you think of the perfect thing to say after the moment has passed. That's one reason it did not get said, however, sometimes you lack the confidence to express your opinion, or the strength to hold onto your point of view.

It is impossible to be made a victim once you know that you are one! If there is anyone bullying you into silence, be silent no more. Once you know that you are a victim and you continue to behave the same way, you are no longer a victim... you've become a volunteer!

Speak up! Stand up for what is important to you... particularly stand up and tell folks how you would like to be treated. You teach people how to treat you, so, if you want to be treated differently, SAY SO!

Let people know who you are and what you stand for—what you value, what you care about. Give people the opportunity to know who you are!

Discipline...

Discipline is the bridge between goals and accomplishment. — Jim Rohn

For most people, the word "discipline" has an immediate negative connotation. It implies something imposed from the outside. It means that someone or something is controlling or demanding. When you do think about self-discipline, it, too, often has a negative spin because it is seen as difficult and contributing to failure. Can you think about it differently?

Self-discipline is nothing more than keeping your commitments to yourself. If you say something is important and significant to you, then take this little test: Does that something that you SAY is important show up a significant number of times in either your calendar, or your checkbook, or both? If it does not, then, where is the demonstration that it is important to you? Do you regularly do what you say has value to you?

Self-discipline arises from self-esteem and self-esteem is enhanced by self-discipline. Do you believe that you are worth spending time and/or money on? Do you get the "left-overs" of time and resources rather than filling your own cup first? It is not unusual to feel that you are being a "good" person when you are self-sacrificing. That's because society often tells you this is so. Oh, good thinking! The society says so because everyone else benefits from your self-sacrifice. In fact, "sacrifice" itself is an interesting concept. The dictionary says it means "the act of giving up or destroying one thing for the sake of something else". Do you really want to be SELF-sacrificing?

Think about any lifestyle changes you would like to make. Make a plan to use your time, money, energy and other resources in ways that reflect what is important and significant to you. You may need to spend time first exploring just what those things really, really are for you.

The problem is never how to get new, innovative thoughts into your mind, but how to get old ones out. — Dee Hock, Founder, VISA

Do you act on your innovative thoughts? Do you at least record them so they are not lost? When you record them, do you spend some time considering their personal importance and viability?

Do you sometimes give away your ideas just because you would like to see them realized or because someone else might benefit? Some folks have been taught to hold tight to their good ideas, keep them "close to their chests".

If you cannot work with all your innovative thoughts, you might hire someone to do it for you. Then you can use your "real" time for creativity and for investing in your highest priorities, while still realizing your other productive ideas with the help of others. This can be extremely profitable in both senses of the word!

Begin an "ideas log". Carry a small notebook and capture your great ideas. Decide to spend time reviewing your log regularly. Save your thoughts!

The Difference...

Often the difference between a success and a failure is not one's better abilities or ideas, but the courage that one has to bet on his [her] ideas, to take a calculated risk—and to act. — Maxwell Maltz

Have you ever made a conscious decision to invest in yourself? To take whatever time, money or other resources you have and give yourself the opportunity you desire? Have you ever had the experience of being willing to give or spend for another person but not for yourself? What is that about?

Each person has a unique contribution to make to this world. That unique contribution may be to be an excellent parent, a great friend, a successful businessperson, to build a fine building, or, perhaps, find a cure for cancer. No contribution is greater than another. Each is valuable and needed. Each person, though, has to decide on the gift they have to give...and value it! Sometimes in seminars, people tell me that there is nothing special about them...they are just "ordinary". Remember, you do not have to be extraordinary, just do the things you do extraordinarily well!

You've probably heard it said that 'the devil is in the details'. How about reframing that to say that excellence is in the details? What would it take for you to be excellent...no matter where you choose to shine? What can you do to lift your contribution from ordinary to extraordinary? Remember, think small...think details...just for today.

Observe what you are doing at any given moment today and ask yourself, "How could I do this just a little (or a lot) better?" Could you brush your teeth a little better? Spend an extra minute with a colleague? Beautify your space? Improve your self-talk? Make a few small post-its and place them in key spots to remind yourself that "Excellence is in the details".

Notice how you feel when you make the extra effort.

Demonstrate Compassion...

Treat every person with kindness and respect, even those who are rude to you. Remember that you show compassion to others not because of who they are but because of who you are. — Andrew T. Somers

You know that the only person you can change is yourself. You can influence, guide, lead and, even, threaten, however, you cannot do the changing for anyone else.

Every moment you draw breath you are modeling what you believe, what you assume, what you value. We are human beings not human "doings". The "doing" is the demonstration of our "being". This is an awesome responsibility.

What are you demonstrating right now by reading this? Hopefully, these quotes and tips are an oasis—a place to stop, to nurture, refresh and re-energize you as you continue on your highest and best path. Reading them demonstrates your caring for yourself and your intention to contribute your best!

...Demonstrate Compassion

Today ask yourself every fifteen minutes or so, "What am I demonstrating by what I am doing or saying right now?" If you are not doing what you value, consider making some changes. If you are doing things that are important, significant and valuable to you, proceed with the assurance that you are on the right path.

Don't Sit Back...

...People of accomplishment rarely sat back and let things happen to them. They went out and happened to things. — Elinor Smith

Are you 'happening'? That's such a great phrase from the younger generations! Are you 'with it'? Hip? On top of it? Part of the action? Are you 'with the program'?

Older generations, particularly the World War II or Silent Generation, began their working careers in a time when there was a strong work ethic, which rewarded loyalty, longevity and servitude. Generation X has a different approach: What's in it for me? Where will it get me? And, now, Generation Y is entering the picture wanting strong relationship possibilities in the work place. Yes, this is a very quick overview of these outlooks, however, they impact the market place and the home strongly. None of these is right or wrong, simply different approaches rising from different economic times.

The truth is that no one can afford to sit back and wait for the world to beat a path to his or her door. It will not happen unless there has been a great deal of effort put into building and maintaining that path! So, get happening!

Spend a few minutes reflecting on your level of outreach for what you want. Are there any places where you could stretch a little more in the direction of your goals? Is there anywhere in your life where you are taking a 'sit back and wait for it to come to me' attitude? If so, why not go after what you want? Do what you can to make it happen.

Soaring...

One can never consent to creep when one feels the impulse to soar.
— Helen Keller

Most relationships in life require your consent, don't they? You consent, or dissent, in many ways. Sometimes you give your consent externally while dissenting internally. This brings you neither integrity, nor peace.

When someone tells a joke that offends you, do you say something about your view? At a minimum, do you refrain from laughing? When someone includes a racial slur in their conversation with you, do you let them know your view? How do you express your consent or dissent? I am not suggesting that you lose your sense of humor, of course. Some turns of phrase are clever, humorous and edgy, and you enjoy those things about them, however, if and when something does offend you, it is worthwhile...and honest...to say something. If you don't, the behavior will continue, won't it? Why? Because, by not saying anything you have given your consent.

You teach people how to treat you. Speak up and tell another person how you want to be treated—what pleases you, what displeases you, what you will tolerate and what you will not tolerate. Relationships become more respectful and more honest. If you do things that please others and not yourself, a dishonest relationship is being created. Tell your truth.

Practice truth in relationship, speak up and let others really know you. John Powell says that: "The genius of good communication lies in being totally honest and totally kind at the same time."

Formula For Success...

If A = success, the formula is A = X + Y + Z with X being work, Y being play and Z, keeping your mouth shut. — Albert Einstein

Have you ever kicked yourself for saying something that would have been better left unsaid? That internal voice was whispering, or screaming, "Don't Do It!", and yet, out it came? You knew better. You said it. You regret it. If you had held your tongue, that conversation may have been more productive. This apparently must have also happened to Einstein. Isn't that reassuring?

You've likely experienced the regret of the word spoken in anger, revenge or thoughtlessness. By saying those fated words, you escalate the conversation. The tone changes. The issue becomes broader, usually more personally offensive and more emotionally charged. This leads you astray from the one point you wished to raise. Escalation goes from the single-point beginning to the multi-pronged assault. Now, instead of one issue to resolve, you have ten. That takes a great deal of backtracking, apologizing…and decompression time. Trust is eroded and feelings are hurt. This is what I call a 'tem-for-one' conversation. It will create fodder for ten more conversations!

Einstein was right. Keeping your mouth shut when emotions are high can be very successful…even if difficult!

Stop and take a breath before you say those words that you really know may take you into a 'ten-for-one' conversation. Be curious. Ask for more information. Truly listen and intend to learn something about the other person. This has a way of changing relationships for the better. Thanks, Albert!

Self-Love...

Self-love is not so vile a sin as self-neglecting. — William Shakespeare

When was the last time you took yourself out to do something that you really wanted to do? If it was during the last week, congratulations! If it was in the last month, good for you. Sometimes we do not want to do things alone, which is understandable. Some things are terrific to share. What, though, if no one comes along to share those special things with you? Are you never going to do them?

Taking good care of yourself is so important for your self-esteem and self-confidence. That includes taking yourself out and doing things you enjoy, too. Have you taken yourself to the movies? That is surely one place that one can comfortably go alone, isn't it? Just you, a big box of popcorn, an outrageously priced soda pop — and a hundred of your closest strangers. Even if you have someone with you, you watch the picture without talking. Do you take yourself for a walk? Do you go to a museum or art gallery? Do you sit by the water and relax? Even if you have a life partner, there are going to be things that he or she does not enjoy but that you do.

Do things because they bring YOU pleasure? Taking good care of yourself in every way is a very positive kind of "selfishness". It fills you up with good things to share with the other folks in your life...including a very good mood.

Think about something you have wanted to do for quite a while—anything, from a long, hot soak in the tub to your first skydive. If you have been putting off doing it because there's no one to do it with, make a plan to do it anyway. Be good to yourself. Take yourself out.

Frustrations...

You must have long range goals to keep you from being frustrated by short-range failure. — Charles Noble

Thomas Edison was very clear that there really was no such thing as failure as he labored to create the first light bulb. He contended that each trial that did not produce a workable model was one more learning; more information about what would not lead him to his desired destination. A very positive fellow, Mr. Edison. Now we call his decision to change his perception, reframing—putting an old view in a new frame. This is a VERY useful technique for you to use as well.

When you are clear where you are headed, you continue to go there even if you take a few detours. The detours may slow the journey down but the usually teach you something, too. The scenery may be appealing, tempting parking spots on the way to success. The trick, of course, is to not let the detour take your eyes off your prize! If you can remember to only stop for coffee on the detour, not build a condo and move in, you'll achieve your goals and experience a new level of self-esteem.

Reflect on places you may be comfortably-or even, uncomfortably parked on the journey to your goals. Is it time to get moving? Do you need to re-focus on the destination or remind yourself why you chose it? Become a traveler again.

Your Battle Cry...

If quality is your goal, then, persistence must be your battle cry.
— Lee Rich

Would you say that you are having a quality life? . Everyone has the right to decide what a 'quality life' is for themselves. You have that opportunity right now.

Your decisions may not be popular in your circle of friends, colleagues or family. As you move into doing things in ways that demonstrate what is important to you, others may not understand. Persist. You are living your life for you, not for them.

This is not a suggestion to be disrespectful to others, but rather, to respect yourself. Some folks do things because that is the way it's always been done. They do things because others expect them to. A quality life comes from respecting what is in your heart, what you want for yourself and what makes sense for you. There could be no quality life for you if you intentionally hurt others by your decisions.

This is an important point. There is a big difference between purposefully hurting others and others being hurt. People can choose to be hurt at any time. Some say they are hurt when you do not do what they want you to do, right? This can also happen when they want to manipulate or influence you by guilt. Guilt trips are neither pleasurable, nor productive. Do not book with that travel agent any more!

Invest an hour in yourself. Decide what you consider to be a quality life for you. What would you do, have and be? How would that be different from what you are doing right now? What would be the first change you would make? What would you do more of? What would you do less of or eliminate completely?

Be gentle with yourself, yet persistent. You deserve to have the quality of life that you most desire. Only you can take those steps. You're important. Do it!

No One To Blame...

Take your life in your own hands and what happens? A terrible thing. No one to blame. — Erica Jong

Do you have any idea how much time you waste in looking for someone to blame? Most folks are good at it because they practice so often.

What would it be like to take 100% responsibility for everything that you are thinking and feeling? What if you made a decision to not spend another moment blaming anyone else for anything?

What it takes is the willingness to "face forward"? You have to be willing to ask yourself, "What do I want from this encounter, circumstance, or person?" and work from there rather than looking backwards to assign guilt or blame. Sure, you learn from your mistakes. We all do. That is not the same thing as looking for someone to blame. You can see what went wrong, analyze what you could have done differently, and move on. That is the concept of blameless error. It happened. What can I learn? What will I change as a result?

Resolve to live without blame. You'll have much more energy for the present moment. You will be happier. What a deal!

Watch your thoughts. Look for patterns of blame that come up as repeated stories from your past. Once you know where you learned a lesson, keep the lesson and let go of the story. Remember, each time you retell a story your body goes through the same emotions as it did when the event first happened. Be kind to your body. Remember the positives and release the negatives.

Declare yourself a "Blame-Free Zone".

Ingredients For Success...

You never become successful by dreaming. You become successful by working to the best of your ability and having faith in yourself. To reach your goal, three main ingredients are necessary—self-discipline, determination and desire. There will always be dark days, but with this foundation, you will be able to face the challenge. — Bernie Parent

Isn't it interesting how advice on achieving success usually comes back to you doing the work? There is no escaping self-discipline. If the very thought of self-discipline causes your stomach to drop, consider this: Self-discipline can be achieved in small increments. Choose something that you truly want to include in your life and do it for only five minutes a day.

Health clubs will tell you that their business sees a significant rise in January. Finding an available machine is difficult. It is not surprising as well-intentioned folks make New Year's Resolutions. They have a desire to be healthier, and are determined to exercise an hour a day. By April, there is often no wait for those same machines. Why? Because folks started out with unrealistic expectations of their ability and willingness to significantly, and immediately, change the way they use their time. Starting out with a half-hour, two or three times a week would have been realistic. As the exercise habit developed, and the results were experienced, desire would increase and self-discipline would be renamed passion. Isn't that appealing?

Choose one thing that you desire to include or increase in your life...and do it for only five minutes. Tomorrow, choose to include it again for only five minutes. Decide each day. See what happens. You may develop a new habit. Take baby steps. It is not the size of the step that counts. It's the willingness to keep walking!

A Light Heart...

A light heart lives long. — William Shakespeare

Are you carrying around old hurts, grudges or stories of pain? Those things are very heavy. They drain your energy and hold you back from being fully present right now. What would it take for you to put them down and carry them no further?

As a psychotherapist, I have spent much time helping folks unpack their heavy baggage and leave it on the roadside. Sometimes that is easier than at other times. Events definitely have different weights and each person's strength to carry them is different. A similar event can have vastly different impact depending on the person and his or her view of it. What seems insignificant to one may be devastating to another. You have probably noticed that.

For that reason, each person's pain must be understood from his/heir point of view. We each see our worlds differently. The good news is that pain can be unpacked. The other good news is that you have choice. You choose whether to carry or put down, whether to focus on the past or be present now, whether to let go or hang on. That is how you acquire a light heart. You choose in favor of yourself and the quality of your life right now. You are in control. If you need help, be sure to get well-qualified help. Choose someone who has two important attributes: expert training AND a life that is working well!

It's not rocket science to realize that the less you carry, the easier the journey. Lighten up!

Do you have an old hurt that weighs you down? Do you have memories of events, issues and people that cause you pain? It is not the memory that you wish to erase, but the negative charge that goes along with it.

Remembering the incident is natural, neutralizing the incident is important. Learn the lesson each event has to teach you and move on. No, it's neither simple nor easy, however, the sooner you do it, the more energy you will have available to you for creating your ideal life right now.

Our Duties...

Our duties are not performed for duties' sake, but because their neglect would make the man uncomfortable. A man performs but one duty—the duty of contenting his spirit, the duty of making himself agreeable to himself. — Mark Twain (who I imagine did know some women and just might have thought that the same idea applies to them!)

You feel good when you have completed a task. Especially if it is one you've been avoiding for a while. You choose your duties just as you choose your pleasures. There is no escape. Life is nothing but choices of one form or another.

How do you content your spirit? Do you know what brings you peace? If you do know, are you engaging in those activities? Do you really believe you deserve to be peaceful and content? If you believe it, you'll do it. Your behavior always gives you away, doesn't it? It does not matter what you say, it's what you do that tells the tale!

How many times do you hear folks tell you that they know _____ would be best for their health? They may even acknowledge that they want good health. Then, what's up with their behavior? The truth is that they want to be busy, comfortable, lazy, pre-occupied, stressed, complaining or guilty MORE than they want to be healthy. If you recognize yourself in that statement, you just may want to sit down, recover, and make a plan to match your behavior to your goals!

Invest an hour imagining how you would feel if you were living your ideal life. Take the time to see, hear, feel, touch, taste and smell that ideal life. Then, choose one area of the ideal and decide to do something that clearly moves you towards it. Just one! Prove to yourself you can do it. Make it very realistic and 'do-able'. Begin that way and soon you'll be picking up speed towards your ideal.

Be Amazing...

Don't be afraid to be amazing. — Andy Offutt Irwin

Do you ever amaze yourself with your creativity, resiliency and willingness? You probably have done amazing things in your life. You've lived through difficult situations, root canals, and losses and you're still standing. Isn't that an amazing example of survival? Sure it is.

Have you recently taken up a completely new hobby, exercise or favorite author? Have you immersed yourself in something new? What's next for you?

Choose something that has caught your eye over the last couple of years and pay attention to it. Would you like to know more about it or do more of it? Could you start now? If you could not do it right now, could you put in place a plan that would allow you to do it in the next few months?

Stretch. Just enough stretch to reach out of your comfort zone, without reaching further than your safety zone! Go for it! Be amazing.

Think back to your early teens. What did you most want to do? Have you done it yet? Invest a half hour in dreaming about what would awaken your spirit and let it soar. Let your mind wander without those nagging judgments—"I'm too old", "I'm too young", "I don't have the time", etc. Just notice what would lighten and brighten your heart. Pay attention. Write a few things down and see if they still sound good next week. If so, start.

Best Routine...

For all my good intentions, there are days when things go wrong or I fall into old habits. When things are not going well, when I'm grumpy or mad, I'll realize that I've not been paying attention to my soul or following my best routine. — Robert Fulghum

Do you know what your best routine is? Do you know what foods make you feel best? Chocolate, perhaps? Have you experimented to find the diet that keeps you energetic, clear-headed and healthy? Do you know what number of hours of sleep is best for you? Do you know how much time you need to spend alone to feel refreshed and in touch with yourself? Do you pay attention to your need to be creative? To play? To accomplish? To laugh? To cry? To talk with friends? To work?

Often your pre-programmed tape begins to run at that point. You know the one that tries to stop you by telling you that you are "too young, too old, too tall, too short, too inexperienced, too far away, too involved, too busy, too _______" to have what you want. Often folks believe that if they lost or gained twenty pounds, cleaned their garages, wrote thank-you notes on time, got out of debt, and ran a marathon that then they would magically meet their life partners and create wealth. Do you have list of things that must be in place before you can have what you want?

Do you want it seriously enough to remove the obstacles? If so, start immediately. Why wait for Monday? Embark on your best routine!

Use a few minutes to reflect on the first thing that comes to mind when you ask yourself what you really want in life. What are you doing to have this become a reality for you? If you truly want it, decide on one thing that you can take action on right away and begin.

If you believe in your dream, if you are passionate about it and keep it uppermost in your mind, you will achieve it.

Remember, what you pay attention to expands!

Go Far From Shore...

Take a chance. All life is a chance. The man who goes the furthest is generally the one who is willing to do and dare. The sure thing boat never gets far from shore. — Dale Carnegie

It used to be that a sense of security could be found in a job. Forty years ago it was common to choose a career, enter at the bottom level, work your way to the top and stay until you retire. A simple formula. The only element of chance was when you made your career choice. After a little initial shuffling, you settled in the company for the long haul.

Now, in the United States, there is so much opportunity that folks are highly mobile, changing jobs easily. Baby Boomers have some difficulty accepting the fluidity of their work forces. Generation X'ers take it in their stride and Generation Y thinks it's the way things are done. Interestingly enough, one ingredient in this shift among generations is that younger people are more relationship-oriented than security-driven. They want to work in places that value team members. They are willing to push off from shore in search of what fulfills them. Are you?

It may be time to re-think the security issue. Are you doing what you love to do? Are there things you have always wanted to do and continue to put off? Why is that?

If you have been staying close to shore, you might want to push off now—or, at least, take a few swimming lessons!

Most folks are very good at self-deception. They have good "reasons" why they do not do what they say they want to do. They surround themselves with folks who will 'buy" their reasons. That way everyone thinks they are comfortable.

Do you have any stock "reasons" for not living your dreams? Think about it. Only you can hold yourself back from the life you really want.

Cut Your Conscience...

I cannot and will not cut my conscience to fit this year's fashions.
— Lillian Hellman

What do you think about the concept of the "little white lie"? You know, the times when you do not tell quite the whole truth, or say something suitably ambiguous so the listener can interpret your words his or her own way. How does it feel to deliver one? Does it affect you any more if you do tell one? What do you tell yourself about it?

If you we say we value honesty and integrity, these little white lies deserve some attention, don't they? We have even developed a word to downgrade them somewhat from real lies. We call them "fibs". The dictionary says a fib is a trivial or childish lie. Now that enters a whole new area of oxymoronic thinking...a trivial lie!

A good friend calls and invites you to a product party. You have a quick contest in your mind regarding the value of the friendship and your desire not to participate. If you decide not to go, can you tell your friend the reason why directly? Or does it require a quick story about previous plans? Or...a little white lie?

Living in integrity is living in accordance with what is most important to you. Does the fact that you both know that the truth is not fully told make it OK? Or do you feel a little twinge each this happens? To eliminate "twinging", practice telling the truth in ways that honor both you and your friend. Yes, sure, it is a little thing...but, then, what else is daily life composed of?

For today, notice or reflect on times when you said something that was not wholly truthful. Did you have some low-level (or high level, for that matter) anxiety about the truth coming out? What is OK —and not OK— with you around telling those little 'white' social lies?

I have noticed that nothing I have never said ever did me any harm.
— Calvin Coolidge

Everyone has had times when their fondest wish would be to re-capture the words they have already spoken. It really does not help to apologize when things said have hurt another. The apology is necessary if it is genuine, but the words have still hit their mark. Restraint is the better option, isn't it?

Have you ever thought about the necessity for and the impact of your words each day? Try this experiment. Spend an afternoon in silence while surrounded by the usual people and activities of the day. Just tell folks about your choice so they understand. Then, notice what you would have said if you had been speaking. You'll likely find that very instructional. There are some traditions that suggest a day's silence each week. There's wisdom there!

If silence is not your preferred option, try this: Before you say anything, say it over once in your head and see how it will play. If it still feels like a positive or necessary contribution, proceed. If not, refrain. You may save yourself many further words of explanation by this practice.

Try eliminating the word "should" from your vocabulary. Replace it with "could" and notice the difference. Most things are options, aren't they? Don't let anyone "should" on you, either!

The Starting Point...

The starting point of all achievement is desire. Keep this constantly in mind. Weak desire brings weak results just as a small amount of fire makes a small amount of heat. — Napoleon Hill

If you picked up that fateful bottle on the beach, and that weary genie popped out to grant you one wish, what would you wish for? Now aside from the mega-wishes like world peace, what do you want most in your life? Do you really know?

You know that you cannot work towards something you cannot name, don't you? Not only do you have to name it but you must name it clearly. Words like 'good', 'nice' and 'comfortable' have no meaning when you are creating your intentions. It's no use saying that you want to be a 'good' parent unless you know how you measure it. Be specific.

If you notice right now that you are saying, "Yes, yes, I know." and letting these thoughts wash over and past you, stop for a moment. You think you know what you mean when you say generalities. Your subconscious mind does not know. It works in pictures and needs clear instructions to create those pictures.

Just like Olympic athletes, you can accomplish your goals when they can be clearly visualized repeatedly. See yourself jumping over your own fifteen-foot pole vault bar. You define the bar, see it clearly and see, feel, hear, taste and smell victory. Then, it will be yours.

Use a half hour today to build the most powerful picture, in your mind, of what you want. When children draw pictures, they often leave a lot of white space—space with nothing in it that could be filled with anything. Leave no white spaces in your picture. Fill in every detail including how you will feel when you have accomplished your goal. Try it. It works.

Do not be embarrassed by your mistakes. Nothing can teach us better than our understanding of them. This is one of the best ways of self-education. — Thomas Carlyle

Every single day you are engaged in self-education. You see things, feel things, react to things, and, hopefully, learn from things. You make decisions that seem right at the time and turn out to be opportunities to decide differently. That is self-education.

It is also self-monitoring, self-directing and self-motivating. These are components of healthy adult behavior, aren't they? I believe an emotional grown-up is a person who is not looking for someone to blame for his or her behavior or choices. Choose good friends and mentors. You can discuss your thoughts, feelings, issues and plans with them, and, then, make your own decision.

There is a feedback system at work all the time in this world. Everything has a consequence. Make your choices with the consequence in mind. Each consequence simply gives you more information for making your next choice.

Reflect on how you make decisions in your life. Are you taking the wonderful opportunity of consciously making your own decisions? Or, as John Lennon asked, "Is life what is happening to you when you are busy making other plans?"

Always Do Right...

Always do right; this will gratify some people and astonish the rest.
— Mark Twain

The best choices are to do what is right, and to do what is right for you simultaneously. Hopefully, these are the same things. Sometimes, though, doing what is right requires some mental gymnastics. You know in your heart it is the right thing to do, but your mind is rationalizing another path as quickly as it can.

So, what is right action for you? When a decision has to be made, do you know the right choice for you? It will be the one where, once it is made, you have no qualms, regrets, or anxiety. Sure, you may play, "I wonder what would have happened if...." a little. In your heart, though, you are smiling. It may take tenacity, and you know it was worth it. It may be unpopular, and, you know it is right. It will sometimes take courage, and, it will bring you a sense of peace. Then you know what right action is.

A colleague put it this way: Right action is when the right people do the right thing for the right reasons at the right time. That about sums it up, doesn't it? How are you doing?

How do you know when all is "right" with your world? Think about times in your life when you have taken the wrong path. How much energy did you spend in regret, anxiety, concern or fear following that decision? Now, think of a time when you made a tough "right" choice for you. What were the deciding factors? How did you feel afterwards?

Which path do you prefer?

Display Character...

Show class, have pride, and display character. If you do, winning takes care of itself. — Coach Paul "Bear" Bryant

Do you take the high road in life? Do you take the right road, rather than just the easy road? Of course, it is perfect when things are both right and easy, isn't it? The trick is to make "doing right" easy!

How do you do that? Here's one way: make a list of the five most important things to you in your life. You might mention your family, your health, your career goal. These are the "non-negotiables" in your life—no matter what, these are the places that will get your attention and energy. Now, for three weeks, practice saying "no" to anything that is not on that list. Just notice the results! You will likely be quite surprised by the freedom, clarity and energy you gain from this exercise. Believe me, the world will not stop turning if you say no. After all, you're only going to do it for three weeks, right?

Being clear about what is most important to you is key. Make that list right now. Now, if you just said to yourself, "That's a good idea. I'll do that later.", notice that. Make an appointment with yourself. Decide right now when you will spend the time to achieve clarity about what you value. You would not dismiss an appointment with an important client or medical specialist, would you? Well, you are more important to you than those other folks. Keep your appointment with yourself! Take time to have the life you want.

Keep a special notebook to record your values, visions, dreams, plans and accomplishments. Make it one that you enjoy looking at and holding. You may have a certain kind of pen that you most enjoy writing with. Keep it with the notebook. Now, make a date with yourself, your notebook and pen—and keep it! It is too easy to think this is a great idea...and never do it!

Have Some Fun!

Unless each day can be looked back upon by an individual as one in which he (she) has had some fun, some joy, some real satisfaction, that day is a loss. — Dwight David Eisenhower

Do you have fun, joy and satisfaction in each day? Do you plan for it? You can, you know.

Do you know what brings you fun, joy and satisfaction? That's the first step. Look for the small things, the things that can be done in an hour or less. Look for the smaller things, too. There are things that just looking at or hearing brings you a good feeling. A client of mine really enjoyed having fresh flowers in her office. We coupled that joy with her feeling of satisfaction when her desk was clear and tasks were well ordered. She put the flowers on her desk as a statement and a reminder that she was in charge of creating those good feelings. Simple, but effective. Beautiful flowers and messy desks just do not go together well.

Do you stay in touch with the people you feel close to? There's another way to bring warmth into your day. Call or write to someone you care about. Take five minutes and connect. Even if you have to leave a message, you have let that person know they are important. Take time to send an email. What could be quicker! Stay in touch with the people and feelings that nurture and nourish you. That's entirely within your control. Give yourself that gift.

Make a list of the most important people in your life. Do those folks know how important they are to you? Is there a mentor, teacher, friend or relative who has touched your life in a special way, no matter how long ago? Send them a note and thank them.

Is there one thing you can give yourself—time, object, experience—that reminds you that you are special and deserving of good care? Put something in your work environment that reminds you to relax, to take good care of yourself, to take a few deep breaths and appreciate.

It may be obvious that you'll never have this day again, but, do you live as though that is true?

Celebrate All Successes...

Jealousy is the tribute mediocrity pays to genius. — Fulton Sheen

You've probably heard or said, "That's just sour grapes", haven't you? We say that when someone will not be happy for another's success because they themselves are not receiving or achieving in the same way. It comes from Aesop's Fable about the fox who could not reach a lovely bunch of grapes hanging too high on a branch, so he sulked away, declaring that they were probably sour anyway. Diminishing the joy or impact of the accomplishments of another is a poor attempt at improving one's own life, isn't it?

Being genuinely happy for the successes of another person adds joy to our day. If one person succeeds, it demonstrates to us all that success is possible. Each time a friend, colleague...or totally unknown person on the other side of the earth, learns, discovers, achieves, or triumphs; it reminds you that you are capable of the same thing. It gives a lift to your day!

If this is difficult for you, it might be time to examine what holds you back from wholeheartedly celebrating with others. Taking the time to do this frees you to experience more joy.

Pay special attention to someone in your life who has something to celebrate. Call them, send them a card or e-mail, and celebrate with them. Here's a hint, too: Even if you have already acknowledged their "win", do it again. We all appreciate recognition.

Change...

Our object in traveling should be, not to gratify curiosity, and seek mere temporary amusement, but to learn, and to venerate, to improve the understanding and the heart. — Gresley

Traveling to foreign countries is a fine way to broaden your understanding of yourself. It is surprising to hear other travelers complaining that 'things are not like they are at home'! If they wanted them to be the same as at home, why did they travel?

Each traveler chooses where attention is placed. Are you open to new experiences? Do you have space in your life and mind to entertain new ideas and possibilities? This can be as simple as trying new foods or learning a new hobby. Of course, it can be as life altering as changing careers, countries or lifestyles, too.

Change keeps you flexible, doesn't it? It keeps your mind from 'freezing' and this has to be a good thing. Change can be inspiring, especially when you choose the change.

How comfortable are you with change? Ancient wisdom reminds us that change is the only permanent thing in life. If that is so...and it certainly seems to be...does it make sense to work hard at keeping things the same? Do you need to review your approach to change?

Now would be a good time to think about this.

Your attitude shapes your experience of your world. Take a few minutes to examine your attitude towards change. Do you embrace new experiences and welcome new ideas? Have you changed your mind recently? How do you perceive others who live differently from you? Are they wrong or just different? When someone you know well chooses to do something unexpected, what is your view of that?

How open are you to change?

Can You Handle It?

The more you love and respect yourself, the more difficult it is for irritating, mean-spirited people to want to be with you. Can you handle the loss? — Harvey Cohen

How do you demonstrate that you respect yourself? Do you speak well of yourself? Do you take good care of yourself in every way? Do you have firm boundaries and express them well when necessary?

Many folks have habits that serve them poorly. One of these is to put yourself down. Yes, it even counts when there is no one around to hear you...even when you're saying it inside your head! You may have a habit of saying something like, "I'm so stupid." or "I'm so clumsy" or the like. If that is so, make a conscious effort to replace those words with words of encouragement for yourself. Remember the maxim: Never say about yourself anything that you do not want to be true. Even when you're alone...

Taking good care of yourself is essential. Who else is going to do it for you, anyway? Sorry, there is no magic here. Only you can give your body, mind and spirit what it needs to be healthy, nourished and nurtured. Do you deserve to be healthy, happy and prosperous?

Can You Handle It?

Here's a thought: Before you do or say anything, ask yourself, "Does what I am about to say or do demonstrate that I love myself and live by my values?"

If so, proceed with assurance.
If not, you've given yourself the opportunity to choose differently!

Grow Your Mind...

The growth of the human mind is still high adventure, in many ways the highest adventure on earth. — Norman Cousins

Are you learning? Do you purposefully expand your knowledge? Do you keep your mind open for possibilities? This may be one of the great indicators of longevity with a clear mind. Recent research suggests that folks who are always learning have far less chance of experiencing dementia in advancing years. That's good news, isn't it?

Closed minds often indicate fearful owners. To entertain new ideas or to enjoy challenges to your opinions and beliefs keeps your mind active. As a by-product, it also keeps your heart beating!

Flexibility in your thinking leaves room for creativity, too. Being unwilling to consider new options or conflicting opinions suggests a lack of security about your current position. Haven't you spoken to folks who have absolutely no space in their thinking for your ideas? These folks think they have the only 'right' idea, opinion or insight. In fact, they are willing to argue that their truth is a little more true than yours! This doesn't make sense, does it?

Open your mind and engage in dialogue. Not only might you learn more, but you might well gain perspective. Stretch your thinking. Growing your mind is truly high adventure. Are you willing to step firmly into mid-air in your thinking?

...Grow Your Mind

Do you have an opinion or belief that you will not explore? Do you listen to the opinions and beliefs of others with an open mind? Be willing to consider possibilities. Play with them. Challenge them, but DO entertain them. This way you will learn, and have the opportunity to change your mind, or confirm your beliefs. Be open. Closed, rigid thinking stunts your growth.

Giving Up Boredom...

In order to live freely and happily, you must sacrifice boredom. It is not always an easy sacrifice. — Richard Bach

You hear a lot about boredom these days—people bored on the job, teens bored with their lives, children bored without a computer or TV screen in front of them. Whatever happened to creativity and "amuse yourself"?

Did you know that boredom causes something called "deprivational stress"? This type of stress can be equally as difficult to manage as that caused by having too much to do. Again, the necessity for keeping your life well-balanced becomes obvious. Too much stress is unhealthy. Too little interest in life is unhealthy. Waiting for someone to do something that interests or amuses you makes that other person responsible for your wellness or happiness...or both. There is definitely something wrong with this picture, isn't there?

When my children were growing up, each time one would complain of boredom I would tell them that only the brain-dead are bored. I laugh each time I hear my daughter tell her son the same thing. Being bored is a choice, of course. You can always think about something if you cannot think of something to do!

Notice your level of curiosity, interest and creativity in all that you do. I cannot imagine that folks interested in optimal living would allow themselves to be bored. We each have the opportunity to create value for ourselves in every moment of our day. It is even possible to do it in a "boring" meeting, film or conversation. Challenge yourself to find the value wherever you are.

Resourcefulness...

Now is no time to think of what you do not have. Think of what you can do with what there is. — Ernest Hemingway

Recently a good friend was telling me that she was about to commit to a network marketing company and that she was sure that she had found the perfect career. It was terrific to hear the certainty in her voice. She went on, however, to tell me that now, before even signing the paper to begin, she needed a new apartment with a separate room for an office, a fax machine, a new printer and other office fixtures. Why? Because, to her, this was what it would take to be successful. I suggested that small steps might be more empowering than large debt...perhaps she could use the things she has until growth is warranted.

Have you ever had the experience of thinking that you cannot begin a project until you have everything that you could possibly need before you start?

What could you do right now with the things you have at hand? What changes could you make in your life right now just by deciding to do so? You do not have to wait until you lose twenty pounds, clean out your basement and garages, and take back your library books, to move yourself forward, although those three things make admirable beginnings, too.

If you find yourself saying, "I would like to do that if only I had _______ or if only I was _____"...change your focus.

What steps could you take right now towards what you want to bring into your life using your present skills, talents, desires and resources?

Bouncing...

Success is how high you bounce when you hit bottom. — George Patton

Are things problems or challenges to you? Do your emotions rule the day or point the way? Do you listen to your feelings, acknowledge them, and decide to do life differently so that you will feel better? How long do you allow yourself to be upset before "picking yourself up, dusting yourself off and starting all over again"?

Your feelings are important. They give you feedback about your response to life, your view of life, your expectations, your self-esteem. Denial of your feelings is folly...as is wallowing in them. Use your feelings as feedback, yardsticks, benchmarks for how closely your thoughts and feelings are allied. This may be a tricky concept. Thoughts and feelings can seem to be simultaneous. The two things are definitely intertwined. Which comes first is not as important as which takes precedence in your decision-making. I suggest that your thoughts are more important. Why? Because, what you decide to think or do will create feelings, and deciding differently, creates different feelings. You know, the old "is this cup half full or half empty" stuff. It's all in your perception.

When things are going very well in your life take the time to discover what you are thinking and doing that is helping this along. Sometimes folks spend much time analyzing the negatives and little time understanding the positives. Examine the positives so you can replicate them. You are very powerful. You are very creative. How are you using these strengths in your life?

Spend some time today reflecting and writing in your journal about what you are or were doing, being, thinking, when you were happiest, most successful. What can you do to replicate or maintain that?

Go For The Great...

Don't be afraid to give up the good to go for the great. — Kenny Rogers

Do you know what is possible for you? Do you accept that you have the ability to create the life you say you want? I hope so...because you do. You are powerful.

Would you be willing to leave something that is working for you to move onto something that could work better for you? Are you ready to leave one rung of the ladder to reach for the next one up? Some folks are very uncomfortable with that idea. Security is very important...and having something good feels secure.

Everything you do, say and think has an impact on your ability to create the life you say you want. Sometimes there is a big difference between what you say you want and what you are doing. Why is this? One of two things are so. Either you are unwilling to do what it takes to have the life you say you want, or you do not really want it! Which is true for you? No matter which is true right now, you can change this. Otherwise, you will have to accept the reality that the life you presently have is the one you want! Are you ready to settle, or, are you ready to reach?

Spend five or ten minutes quietly with your eyes closed. Use the time to imagine your ideal life. Picture it vividly. See the colors. Hear the sounds. Even know how it tastes and smells. Imagine how you will feel when this is reality. Do this everyday for a week and notice how you feel. Notice what changes you begin to make in your life, too. It works!

Reflecting...

Tonight when you lay your head on your pillow, forget how far you still have to go. Look instead at how far you've already come. — Bob Moawad

Do you take time to reflect on all that you have learned? Do you give yourself credit for what you have done, what you have journeyed through? This is important.

Some folks have difficulty receiving compliments. You say to them, "I think you look terrific today!" and their response is "What? This old thing? You've got to be kidding." They find it difficult to accept hearing something good about themselves. Receiving a compliment graciously with a "Thank you" is the beginning. Allowing yourself to feel good about receiving it is important. That is what people with high self-esteem and self-confidence do. In fact, that is one way they developed self-esteem and confidence.

Notice your self-talk. Do you notice when you do something well? Do you tell yourself that you did it well? This is not arrogance or conceit. This is self-esteem. There is a big difference. Self-esteem is internal and measured only by you. Arrogance and conceit arise when you think you are superior to others.

A high level of self-esteem comes from noticing what you do well—relationships, parenting, career, community — it comes from focusing on the good in yourself. It gives you self-confidence. Receiving compliments well contributes to this. Take good care of yourself!

Sit down for a half hour alone. Make a list of all the things you do well, all the things you like about yourself. If you have done this before, take out your journal and re-read the list. Add to it, as well.

If you find yourself thinking that you "shouldn't" be so self-centered, correct this thought. It is not self-centered to know what you do well and to appreciate yourself and your accomplishments.
It is polishing your unique gift to give to your world.

Reach High...

Reach high, for stars lie hidden in your soul. Dream deep, for every dream precedes the goal. — Pamela Vaull Starr

What would it mean to you to reach high? Anything worth having is certainly worth stretching for. Stretching means exercise. You will need to exercise your imagination, your vision and your willingness. When you can clearly see what you are reaching for, you can stack up the furniture and climb. If more effort went into moving forward than into creating reasons why not, more would be accomplished.

Accomplishing more is completely defined by you. For some folks, it may mean being more loving, less sarcastic, exercising fifteen minutes a day. For others, it may mean running a marathon, building a new business, and learning to fly an airplane. It is a relative term and you decide what it means. It seems that our world has a less gentle view of it. You are petitioned to do more, be more, spend more, have more with every advertisement you see. Those are choices and each of you has the right and the opportunity to choose what "accomplishing more" means for you. There is no right answer. We all have habits, situations, relationships or careers that can improve. You choose what you are moving forward in your life.

Reaching for the stars may be another way of saying, "Keep on growing!"

Look for places in your life where growth may have slowed down or stopped.

Is that what you want?

If not, make a plan to add water, light and fertilizer and get growing again!

See Beauty...

Youth is happy because it has the ability to see beauty. Anyone who keeps the ability to see beauty never grows old. — Franz Kafka

Do you surround yourself with beauty? What do you see when you open your eyes each morning? When you look at something or someone, do you look for the beauty? These are choices, aren't they? You can focus on whatever you choose at any time.

One way that you can demonstrate your caring for yourself is to arrange your living space in ways you find beautiful. This will help you feel refreshed and re-energized, AND, it will help you to feel taken care of, too! It's wise to remember that pampering yourself is a gift you give to others. Does that sound paradoxical? Well, when you are well taken care of, you have much more to give. You feel better and that is reflected in your relationships. Taking good care of yourself is not selfish. It is wise.

Look for beauty in everything. That's another approach to 'catching them doing it right'! Look for the positive, the useful, the unique, the special in everything. No, it's not a 'Pollyanna' approach to life. It will not remove your good judgment and intuition. It will lift your mood, your sense of well-being and your relationships to a higher level. That has to be beautiful!

Write yourself a memo about beauty. How will you focus on bringing it into your life? What will you do to see beauty first thing in the morning? If 'beauty' is not a comfortable word for you, just change it. You may prefer 'pretty', 'classic', 'organized', 'functional', 'inspirational'—these may be beautiful to you. The point is to consciously take action to focus on the things that make you feel that all is right with your world. Treat yourself well. Start right away.

Look Fear In The Face...

You gain strength, courage and confidence by every experience in which you really stop to look fear in the face. You must do the thing which you think you cannot do. — Eleanor Roosevelt

Often, we hear folks say that they would love to do, have or be something, followed immediately by "I could/would, if only...". If you have said this, what followed the "if only"? Humans are creatures of habit. Psychology tells us that it takes a minimum of 21 consecutive days to create a new habit and/or replace an old habit. It could be possible that your "if only" is a habit of thought could be changed by your decision to think differently.

Sometimes life takes a role of teacher and creates circumstances in which you learn that you CAN do what you thought you could not do. Why wait? If you really want something, then the best first step is to see, hear, smell, taste and feel it as already present, and, then, do everything you can think of to do to bring it into reality.

Focus on what you want, then write down every single thing you can think of that you might have to do in order to get it. Review your list. If there is anything on your list that you are truly unwilling to do, then modify the goal. Why? Because your unwillingness to do whatever it takes will impede the process.

...Look Fear In The Face

Take two of your major goals and list all the things you might have to do to attain them. If there is anything that you are unwilling to do, even if it is unlikely that you would have to do them, alter your goal. To achieve something, you have to be willing to do whatever it takes.

Adversity...

Kites rise highest against the wind-not with it. — Winston Churchill

When life seems to handing you lemons, make lemonade! That would be a more current version of Churchill's quote, wouldn't it? It seems that you often take adversity as an indication that you're going in the wrong direction, or that you don't have what it takes to make it, or that "somebody up there doesn't like you". This is a straightforward cause-and-effect approach that can stop you in your tracks and leave you sitting there for days, months, years or, for some, a lifetime.

What is your approach to adversity? Does it cause you to reflect on your direction and look for alternatives? Does it strengthen your resolve to continue? Does it beat you down and flatten you out? Your responses to life are your choice. There is no escaping the responsibility you have for choosing the way you see things. For some of you, in some circumstances, that choice seems the only one you have any control over…so take it!

When you raise your kite, keep it flying.

Play with the idea of seeing change or difficulties as shifting winds to help your kite stay up... not as an indication that you're flying the wrong one on the wrong day. How can you use the information you are receiving to help the kite climb?

Focus...

Attention is like a searchlight; when its beam is spread over a vast area, its power to focus becomes weak, but focused on one thing at a time, it becomes powerful. Great men [and women] are men [and women] of concentration. They put their whole mind on one thing at a time.
— Paramahansa Yogananda

Did you know that humans are only capable of having one thing on their mind at any one time? The mind has a binary function and, therefore, can only entertain one thought at a time. When our mind is said to be "racing", it is. It is shifting from thought to thought as rapidly as it is capable. The thing to learn, then, is to harness the capability of the mind to focus on one thing and stay focused.

Have you ever begun to work on a project, and had other things pop into your mind that could be done instead. Sometimes these things seem compelling and you do them before even beginning. Examine your choices when you are being distracted. It could be that you are not committed to what you have set yourself to do. With planning, you can train yourself to pay attention to the task at hand! It takes practice... and willingness.

Take the time to remind yourself why you are doing what you are doing at any time. Do things with attention and mindfulness. You will also be clear about how each activity contributes to reaching your goals.

Consistently Yourself...

You cannot consistently perform in a manner which is inconsistent with the way you see yourself. — Zig Ziglar

It's really difficult to pretend all the time, isn't it? It is also really difficult to "rise to an occasion" and sustain the elevation! Mountain climbers train on smaller faces. Do you?

If Zig Ziglar is right, and "you cannot consistently perform in a manner which is inconsistent with the way you see yourself", then, the first step would be to change your view of yourself. Or, at least, your view of what you think is possible for yourself. When you see yourself living the lifestyle you most want and taking active steps to achieve and maintain it, you'll do it. If it is an idle wish, you'll sit around talking about it with other idle wishers. You'll have lots of company, too!

What would it take for you to aim a little higher in life? Just a little higher, to start with. Just like the mountain climber, start on the small hills. You'll notice that the view from the top of them will make the peaks seem more reachable!

Choose just one piece of your life. How would you like to elevate it? What would it take? What are you willing to do? When will you begin? If not now, when? What might stop you from doing it? Plan for overcoming the obstacles and resistances. Then, you will be ready when they show up.

Just choose this one piece of life for now. It will demonstrate to you what you are capable of doing in any area of your life.

Learning From Others...

Human beings, who are almost unique in having the ability to learn from the experience of others, are also remarkable for their apparent disinclination to do so. — Douglas Adams

Do you learn from your own mistakes? That's what they are for, you know. You might not learn the first time, however, each successive time, your learning curve could be a little sharper until you actually remember the lesson before you make the mistake again. Most folks take a while to incorporate their learning into their daily living. Time is not the primary issue, learning is.

Perhaps one of the reasons people enjoy reading quotes from wise, infamous or brilliant people is to wake up their own thinking and learn from others' lessons. You want to be stimulated to think and have that "Aha!" experience without having to go through the pain of the lesson yourself. Reading the quotes often reminds you of what is possible in life and this is comforting as well as challenging. Why do you enjoy reading quotes?

Is there a lesson in your life that seems to be repeating? What is your resistance to learning it? Sometimes it is helpful to read a biography of a person you admire and learn through their experience. You might listen to an interview or watch a video that helps you learn a lesson without the struggle or pain. Shorten your learning curve by using the experience of others. That's wise, isn't it?

Spend some time with a few elderly folks. Ask them what the most important things they have learned are. Use this information to reflect on what you are doing in your life right now and why. Make it a point to chat with folks about their learning and apply it to your own life. Life benefits from some team effort!

Opportunity...

Every situation, properly perceived, becomes an opportunity.
— Helen Schucman

Isn't it wonderful to know how much choice you have in your life? It is such a powerful feeling, isn't it? You choose your perceptions which create your thoughts and your feelings. From those thoughts and feelings, you decide on your actions. Actions have consequences ...and you perceive those consequences and the cycle repeats. You give everything the meaning that it has for you. A very powerful position!

So, what are you doing with this power? Are you accepting the challenge to monitor your perceptions? Are you willing to question your habitual perceptions of yourself, others, situations and events? What would it be like to look at these things with fresh eyes? A new beginning? Perhaps, with a new perspective?

Set aside thirty minutes. Write down all the things that would complete this sentence, "I am...". Do not monitor or assess what you are writing, just capture every single thought. When you think you have exhausted the list, go for five minutes more.

Now, turn the paper over, put the pen or pencil into your other hand, and do the exercise again, in the same way. Again, when you think you have exhausted your thinking, go for five minutes more.

Now, look at your lists. Sure, there will be some items that are the same. What do you notice is the most remarkable difference between the two lists? Create your own insights.

Keeping Your Dreams...

There are many ways of breaking a heart. Stories were full of hearts broken by love, but what really broke a heart was taking away its dream—whatever that dream might be. — Pearl Buck

Some people have dreams. Some people have wishes. Some do not dare to dream. Life is limited only by your willingness to dream and, then, to do whatever it takes to bring the dream to reality. Those who only wish, do have dreams, but they decide those dreams are too big for them and they do nothing about them. That's why they are only wishes.

Of course, you have to believe you deserve to fulfill your dream to make it a reality. That sounds so simple—and it is. It's just not always easy! If you believe in yourself AND you are willing to do whatever is required of you to live that dream, you are very likely to succeed. Keeping the goal in sight, affirming it daily—hourly, if necessary—keeps your passion for it alive!

Very few people have their dreams taken from them. Many give up on their dreams. We have been inspired by the "Dare to Dream" speech and, once we have "dared to dream", we must dare to stay on the path to that dream! That's where integrity lives.

Honestly assess yourself. Do your words and behaviors match? Are you saying you want one thing and behaving as though you want another? If you tell someone you love them, behave in ways that show that. If you tell yourself you deserve to reach your dream, be sure to follow the path that will take you there.

Simplicity...

True simplicity is both buoyant and bountiful, able to liberate depressed spirits from the bondage and burden of extravagance and excess.
— Sarah Ban Breathnach

Do you feel the calmness of a deep breath when you say or hear the word, "simplicity"? Does it conjure up space, serenity, peace and other desirable things? What would it take to bring simplicity into your values?

This world is working hard to make things bigger, faster, newer, complex, convoluted, urgent, anxious and fearful. You have probably noticed that. At the end of a too full day you can feel as though you have been accelerated through a time machine without your consent. The important part, of course, is to notice that you did give your consent; otherwise you would not have done it. This is a beginning realization of your part in creating simplicity.

Is there simplicity in your home? Is there space around things for the air to circulate, or, are pieces of furniture and "things" packed tightly together? Are surfaces clear and spacious? Does every "thing" have a designated spot? Does clutter get taken care of immediately before it becomes an art form? If you have clutter, you are getting in your own way.

Here's a three-part rule my husband and I created: if a thing is beautiful, functional or memorable, it can stay. This rule has a second part. If the things kept have not been appreciated, used or held within twelve months, they have to leave then. This has been a great step toward simplicity.

Survey your surroundings: your home, your room, your office... even just one drawer. Can you simplify it in any way?

Extend this practice as you have time and inclination. It will move you towards a deeper sense of peace and tranquility.

What? Me, Worry?

Let us be of good cheer, remembering that the misfortunes hardest to bear are those which never happen. — James Russell Lowell

This quote is an interesting twist on a useless activity that many people feel is required of them in order to be responsible. That activity is worrying.

I wonder how many teenagers have been brought home safely late at night by a mother staying up and worrying where they are and what they are doing. I wonder how many people have turned around adversity in their lives by wringing their hands, not eating and having insomnia. There is an ethic ingrained in the many of us, that worrying is a virtue...it somehow shows we care deeply about something.

If we could understand another principle, worry would be a thing of the past. It's a simple one: each person has energy to use, you use it in the way you choose, so why choose to use it worrying? When something looms, or occurs, that causes you concern, make a plan to do something about it. Take action! Figure out what will change the situation, or create a positive outcome, and use your energy for that. Take the first, even the smallest, step you can towards solution, rather than waste that energy worrying. Be pro-active, too. Think ahead. Take care of things in a timely manner so that you prevent yourself from creating situations that cause tension.

...What? Me, Worry?

If you find yourself worrying, take a deep breath in through your nose, release the breath slowly through your mouth, and relax. Then ask yourself, what is the first thing I know to do about this to create a positive outcome.... and do it!

Share Good Ideas...

If you share a good idea long enough, it will eventually fall on the ears of good people. — Jim Rohn

What percentage of your time is spent discussing positive things? Are you a late-night news person? Do you know how important your thoughts are...and that you choose them?

When you focus on the good, the preferred, the 'right-for-you' choices, life becomes much brighter. Sure, there are challenges, issues, concerns and complexities. Make your overall focus a positive one, not an unrealistic one. After all, you and you alone choose what you think about and dwell on. Why would you choose the negative? It's a quality of life issue, isn't it?

Share your good ideas, your hopes and dreams. Others may have the resources you want to make those dreams reality. Ask them for their help. There is no great value in doing things alone the hard way. Invite information, insights and ideas. Recruit others to your team. Be on their team, too. Start a Master Mind group** with other like-minded folks. Join one. Surround yourself with folks who are moving forward, and move with them.

Get together with three friends and invest an hour or two in talking about your most important goals. Brainstorm for each other about how to achieve those goals. Who can help whom how and by when? Gather resources. Keep each other in mind. Arrange your next meeting. Keep going!

Discovery...

Discovery is seeing what everybody else has seen, and thinking what nobody else has thought. — Albert Szent-Gyorgi

Have you ever played the game where you take an ordinary object...like a kitchen strainer or a corkscrew...and think of as many things as you can that it could become or be used for? What could it be if it were ten times bigger? Or a hundred times bigger? Or teeny tiny? I'm sure you get the picture. It is an excellent way to start a brainstorming session. It actually comes from the world of drama where it is used to stimulate creativity. The trendy phrase for it just now is "thinking outside the box".

Have you ever done this with decorating? Ask yourself how you could use your possessions in different ways. Which pieces of furniture could be used for different purposes, or in different places or arrangements?

Take a simple dish and find new uses for it. Move your artwork around. Create landscapes on tables, desks, mantels or sills. Play with your surroundings. This, too, stimulates your creativity and costs nothing. At a class I took recently, it was suggested that we go home and move twenty-seven objects in our homes to new places. This was to bring fresh energy to our environment. That might be fun to do and help you see your space in new ways. Refresh your view of the things in your life. Why are they with you? Did you choose them? Do you choose them now? Shake things up a bit and see what happens.

Spend a few minutes with your journal. Write a list of all the lovely things you would like to hear about yourself from other people. Do it with your left hand. Ask your best friend to say one or two of them to you. Better yet. Make your list and ask your best friend to make his/her list. Then share the lists and really enhance your friendship.

Success is the sum of small efforts, repeated day in and day out.
— Robert Collier

Sometimes in life you seem to have to hear the same message many, many times, from many different sources, before you turn it from words into action in your own life. So many times we hear that we are most likely to succeed when we consistently do the right things to reach our goals—and so many times we seem to ignore it!

Think about your desktop or your exercise program. OK, the quote does say "small efforts", however, the occasional flight of stairs doesn't quite make an exercise program, now does it? Nor does that clear space in the very middle of your desk quite make an organized workspace. These are my two areas of greatest challenge. What are yours?

I recently heard an excellent speaker, Allan Weiss, from Rhode Island, who spoke of the 1% solution. He said that if we would improve 1% per day, we would be twice as "good" in seventy days. It makes sense. So often we use the "upheaval approach" to change. That's my term for wanting to change many areas of life at once. Why not try the 1% solution?

Improve one area of your life by 1% today. You may find it so easy that you want to do the same thing tomorrow! Keep track of those improvements here!

Being Your Unique Self...

You do not become someone you're not. In fact, to be successful you have to be yourself. You simply have to "be yourself" more consciously, purposefully, and positively than you may have been in the past.
— D.A. Benton

Do you know the old children's rhyme, "If wishes were horses, beggars would ride; if onions were watches, I'd wear one by my side"? Sometimes we wish we were someone else, and sometimes we try on different ways of being, however, at any moment, no matter what we are doing, we are being ourselves. Quite paradoxical, isn't it? And, there is no escaping it by using the curious phrase "I wasn't really myself when I did that"!

If you want to follow a new career, a new spiritual path or health program, it requires change. Maybe now, there is extensive studying to fill hours previously spent in recreation and relaxation. Maybe now, there is a desire to spend time in meditation and inspirational reading. Maybe now, there is a conscious effort to change eating and exercise patterns. This is purposeful change. These are examples of bringing more consciousness into daily living. Positive changes move you to optimal living.

To become all that you desire to be requires continuous change, continuous growth, however, you never lose yourself in the process because the process itself requires that you become more. You amplify your unique self by living more and more consciously. You see more, feel more, hear more, experience more.

Every half hour, take a conscious, deep breath in through your nose, and release it slowly through your mouth, relaxing your shoulders and neck. As you do this, notice how you are feeling both physically and emotionally. Make a note of what you observe here.

No matter how much time you prefer to spend in the past or the future, the truth is that this is the only time you have. Become more present in every moment in every relationship every day.

Index

1

A

B

C

D

E

H

I

J

K

L

M

N

O

P

Q

R

S

T

About Rhoberta Shaler...

Rhoberta Shaler, PhD, speaks, coaches & conducts seminars for entrepreneurs & professionals who want the motivation, strategies and inspiration to achieve, to lead and to live richly. She has spent over 30 years teaching, encouraging and inspiring thousands of people to look at their personal and corporate lives from a new perspective. Rhoberta challenges them to create integrity between their plans and their daily practices, their beliefs and their behaviors. Her commitment to finding passion in life and pursuing it is contagious.

A Canadian, she currently lives in San Diego, CA, with her husband, Keith Couch. Rhoberta loves to meet new people, go to the theater, read, walk, knit, travel and spend time with her family, friends and colleagues. She is a member of the National Speakers Association.

Presentation Information

Dr. Shaler speaks to thousands of people each year giving them and their organizations 'The OK's to SUCCEED!" --the Optimization Keys to lift their sights and elevate results from acceptable to EXCEPTIONAL.

Her *Living Richly™ Accelerated Achievement Program* and *Living Richly™ Weekends* offer intensive personal development for people ready to take their lives to the next levels. You can sponsor a one-day or two-evening, *Living Richly™ Seminar* in your area. Offer this as a value-added bonus to your members, clients or staff. See the website for details.
www.OptimizeLifeNow.com/LR

Rhoberta's complete press kit is available online. You'll find detailed descriptions of her keynotes and programs, testimonials, client list, biography and photos for booking and media use. You may also call Toll Free in North America 1-877-728-6464 to request more information.

If I could only have ten books to motivate and sustain me, I would choose:

PSYCHO-CYBERNETICS *by Maxwell Maltz, M.D.*

THE ROAD LESS TRAVELED *by M. Scott Peck*

THINK & GROW RICH *by Napoleon Hill*

LOVE IS LETTING GO OF FEAR *by Gerald Jampolsky*

THE MASTER-KEY TO RICHES *by Napoleon Hill*

THE DRAGON DOESN'T LIVE HERE ANYMORE *by Alan Cohen*

MAN'S ETERNAL QUEST *by Paramahansa Yogananda*

FLOW: THE PSYCHOLOGY OF OPTIMAL EXPERIENCE *by Mihaly Csikszentmihalyi*

THE SEAT OF THE SOUL *by Gary Zukav*

THE MAGIC OF THINKING BIG *by David J. Schwartz, PhD*

Give this book to someone you care about!

Share *OPTIMIZE Your Day!* with friends, family and colleagues. Order your copies directly from www.OptimizeLifeNow.com or order it from your favorite online bookseller.

If you would like to order more than 10 copies, a volume discount is available when you order directly from the author at books@OptimizeLifeNow.com

Online for You... All the time...

At Dr. Shaler's websites, you'll find great content you can use today, plus details on her speaking and training topics & programs; valuable, practical tools and strategies for improving work and home relationships; free ezines, articles, tests, interactive games and polls.

www.OptimizeLifeNow.com

Subscribe to these motivating ezines – Free For You From Dr. Shaler's Websites

...for optimal living
Optimize Your Day! Receive further quotes and tips for optimal living right in your email box each week.

... for your personal success
Optimize Life Now! A weekly ezine filled with articles, insights, tips and quotes to help you achieve success on your own terms, create quality relationships and maintain healthy balance.

... for your workplace success
Speaking About Work...™. A bi-weekly journal packed with tips and strategies for improving workplace and client relationships, building and strengthening teams, and managing conflict, anger and difficult people. It's like having a private seminar in your email!

To Book Dr. Shaler to speak at your next event, conference or seminar, visit www.OptimizeLifeNow.com. Download her press kit from the Press Room and contact Jane@OptimizeLifeNow.com

Other Products From Dr. Shaler...

All products can be ordered securely online through Dr. Shaler's website. We accept all major credit cards, online checks, mail and fax orders.

Audio Tapes:

Living Richly™ Eight Essentials for Having the Life You Want – An 8-cassette or 2-CD Seminar

Living Richly™ Home Study Program – An 8-cassette or 2-CD self-directed program with companion workbook

You Are the Mastermind of Your Masterpiece – Make Your Life a Work of Art. Examine your current path and create the life you want.

Be Positively Selfish/Be A Real Goal Getter - Strategies to bridge the gap between goals and measurable results. Get you what you want in life.

Attitudes Heal: Change your way of thinking... change your health.

Cancer Is A Challenge: Strategies for managing through a diagnosis and living beyond it.

Fighting Fires Without Burning Bridges Communication and Conflict Management.

Get Life Lined Up! Responding Well to Change

Visit www.OptimizeLifeNow.com for many other products! Great as gifts for family, friends & colleagues.

Stories, Stars & Sticky Rice: Creating Success on Your Own Terms

Don't Tell Me to Calm Down! Managing Anger - Yours & Theirs

Get Your Ducks in a Row! Encouraging Self-Esteem, Self-Awareness & Self-Confidence in Young Children

Books:

The Handbook to Living Richly™ Eight Essentials to Creating the Life You Most Want

Optimize Your Day! Practical Wisdom for Optimal Living

Keep It In Mind! Memorable Messages for Staying On Track

What You Pay Attention To Expands. Focus your thinking. Change your results.

Prevent Freefall: Pack Your Own Parachute. Timely tactics for taming tense times (booklet)